MW01092593

Praise for
Neglect – The Silent Abuser

In therapy settings, we all talk about trauma, but often we seem to focus on overt events—verbal, physical, and sexual abuse, bullying, serious accidents/illnesses, etc. We seem to forget about the quieter forms of trauma like neglect. And even when we're aware of neglect and its potentially devastating impact, we tend to not recognize its many subtleties. With this much needed book, Enod Gray addresses this shortcoming. This is recommended reading for any person whose childhood was less than perfect.

—**Robert Weiss PhD, MSW, author of** *Prodependence:*
Moving Beyond Codependency

An important book compassionately written by an experienced therapist. Enod Gray moves the reader through an area of human abuse and trauma often overlooked, neglect. Weaving together impactful stories, solid research, and clinical advice, this book will provide clarity, direction, healing and hope. A must read for both therapists and clients alike.

—**Mari A. Lee, LMFT, CSAT-S, author of** *Facing Heartbreak:*
Steps to Recovery for Partners of Sex Addicts, Healing Betrayal,
and The Creative Clinician

The experience and impact of neglect is often overlooked, even by well-meaning counselors and therapists. Consistent neglect renders a person invisible, and its impact can be soul-killing. Enod Gray's work shines a deserving light on the hidden, yet pervasive, experience of neglect in childhood, and offers hope and a path forward for healing.
—**Vicki Tidwell Palmer, author of** *Moving Beyond Betrayal: The 5-Step Boundary Solution for Partners of Sex Addicts*

I was already in awe by chapter one – this book is so good! Neglect adds foundational knowledge and validation to the field of psychology and self-help. Neglect is a gift to anyone who needs to heal from what never happened.
—**Staci Sprout, LICSW, CSAT, author of** *Naked in Public: A Memoir of Recovery from Sex Addiction and Other Temporary Insanities*

What a treasure this book is for clinician and client, alike! Enod Gray has managed to gather up extensive training and research, combine that with her years of experience on the frontlines of treating trauma and addiction, and give us an accessible guide to a one of the most common issues faced in therapy: the treatment of neglect and its effects.
—**Jake Porter, LPC Intern, NCC, CSAT, CMAT, CPC, CCTP, Founder & President, Daring Ventures, Counseling, Coaching and Consulting, LLC**

What I most enjoyed about this thoughtful and thorough book was how I was led to reflect on my own life and relationships. The book is about an immense problem in our culture - that of neglect, of not paying proper attention to those we claim to love. It is also about becoming aware of the neglect we ourselves may have experienced for one reason or another and how that affects our lives now. Enod Gray provides solutions for an aching problem of our time. Read it and then keep it handy. It is a resource for how to have better relationships with Self and others.
—**Dr. Bill Kerley, Th.D, LMFT**

Neglect
THE SILENT ABUSER

How to Recognize and Heal
from Childhood Neglect

ENOD GRAY

Neglect—The Silent Abuser

How to Recognize and Heal from Childhood Neglect

Copyright © December, 2018 Enod Gray

ISBN: 978-1-796827-65-1

Printed in the United States of America

There comes a time when

You have to let everything fall apart.

When you have to stop fighting for a life you've

outgrown and trust that you will be okay, even if you

can't see how right now. For a while everything may

feel messy and hard, and you may feel scared and

lost. Embrace the fear. Embrace the uncertainty.

Embrace the loss. The dark tunnel of change

leads to the light of possibility, but first

you have to go through it.

Lori Deschene

With love and appreciation

This book is dedicated to all the

wounded and neglected clients

Who through their hard work and perseverance

Found the courage to

Take the Heroes' Journey

And found their True Selves.

Acknowledgements

I wish to acknowledge the following people, without whose help this book would not have been written:

Daphne Gray-Grant for holding me accountable and checking on me daily to make sure I made my word count. For patiently cheering me on when I needed a boost,

Gayle Jamail, my former sponsor and now one of my dearest friends, for always believing in me and being there when I needed to talk.

Tami VerHelst for being the first to read my manuscript and liking it!

Scott Brassart, my editor, who was available, encouraging, and professional. Thank you!

Jake Porter for being a supportive and kind friend to me as well as a professional colleague as I went through this book writing process.

Pia Mellody for listening to her Higher Power and bringing Post Induction Training into being. I have used much of her material in this book. She taught me to be a functional adult and to recognize my own inherent worth.

Kathleen Geiger and Sarah Bridge who allowed me to be the client as they worked their Family of Origin intensive on me.

Dr. Bill Kerley who taught me the value of having a daily practice.

Frances J. Harvey, CPC

Carolyn Sheltraw, Cover design and layout

Joan Shapiro, MLS, Indexing

All my precious and courageous clients who entrusted me with their sacred life stories.

Lastly, to my life partner, Terry Harris, who patiently and without complaint was quiet while I spent hours on my computer doing this work.

If I have overlooked anyone, please forgive me.

Table of Contents

Part Three: Healing

Part Four: Steps to Regaining Consciousness

Introduction

THE AWAKENING

"We shall not cease from exploration, and the end of all our exploring will be to arrive where we started and know the place for the first time."
T.S. Eliot

This book is about neglect and the resultant loneliness and isolation that seems to be more and more pervasive. Often it is unrecognized in our individualistic society. We must face the reality that lonely and neglected people do desperate things. Most of the time experiences of neglect and loneliness only serve to instill negative internal beliefs in the individual, establish addictive behaviors, encourage a false persona of "happiness" expressed on the outside, while covering up enormous pain on the inside. But sometimes the pain erupts into behavior(s) that harms others, whether physically or mentally.

In my years of being a psychotherapist, I have noticed again and again clients who report abuse, but fail to notice that they were neglected. If there was no obvious abuse, the neglect goes undetected, except to note that the individual is having trouble with relationships, depression, self-blame and a host of other consequences. It is only when I ask pointed questions aimed at eliciting reflection as to the possibility that the person may have experienced childhood neglect that the truth comes out.

Last year I was in an airport returning from a long flight and waiting at the gate for my flight home. This was the scene I witnessed at the crowded and noisy gate. A father, about 35 years old, was sitting near his portable device which he had just plugged into the charging station. Near him were two children, one about a year old in a stroller and the other about three. Both children were wailing. The man was on his phone-not talking, but reading something. He was oblivious to the cries of his children. About 10 minutes later the mother arrived with a pizza. I thought, "Oh good! She will care for the children." Instead, she shouted to each child, "SHUT UP!" while shoving a portable device (with games on it, presumably) in front of each child. Both continued to whimper, but eventually gave up trying to get their parents' attention and settled down to watch their devices.

I couldn't help but think what might have been different if the father and mother both took the children in their laps and comforted them, offered them something to eat, maybe soothed them to sleep, paid attention to them, instead of leaving that task to the games on their devices. I'm not opposed to the devices at all-what a wonderful invention! However, isn't there a case that even though everyone is tired, that the kids were crying to be noticed and needed comfort? What were the children learning about connection, about life? Who will they be and what will they be like when they grow up?

This book offers information about neglect, the brain, addictions, and specific strategies for recognizing and healing from the trauma neglect produces. If you suspect you may have experienced neglect but are unsure, I recommend you read the personal stories scattered throughout the book as well as the ten types of families that pose a risk of being neglectful. In this way you may be able to recognize patterns of behavior that feel familiar to you.

There is no magic 1-2-3 recipe for being "cured." I wish there were. This book is about your life and Life itself. It is about really being awake and aware of how very precious your life is and learning to appreciate each day, each moment fully. To do that you will have to first of all, wake up and secondly put into place certain practices to give you the best chance possible of achieving your goals and intentions. It is never too late nor is anyone ever too far gone to do this.

Neglect happens to all genders, all sexual orientations, all races and ethnic groups, all socioeconomic groups. Regardless of the pronoun that you see in this book, please change it to fit your situation.

Another thing you will notice is that I have capitalized the word Self. This is deliberate. The word "Self" is referring to that beautiful, precious, divine inner person that you were born to be. Regardless of the circumstances of your birth or the family into which you were born, and regardless of where you are now in your life, I want you to remember every time you see the word "Self" with a capital "S", that you are a noble and unique human being worthy of love and respect. Neglected people tend to downplay their sense of worth. It is time to stop doing that.

Each day builds on itself, until we finally cut through all the fog and strategies we have constructed to guard against the hurtful reality of our childhood.

Healing and hope are possible if you are willing to do the work. Let's get started.

TELLING OUR STORIES

Throughout the book you will find actual stories of clients who have experienced neglect. There are no stories of outrageous overt abuse. I have done this intentionally so that you may see that neglect is very subtle. The behavior in the family may have been highly dysfunctional; however, sometimes it is hard to spot what generally would be referred to as abuse. Please note that fictitious names are used and the circumstances changed to protect confidentiality. All the stories demonstrate examples of how insidious this silent abuser can be and how it affects our adult lives. Included are stories of neglect by abandonment and neglect by overcontrol.

What is the rationale behind talking about what our childhoods were like? There is something about telling our stories that is both daunting and freeing. First, we have to be aware of what was really true. Sometimes, just in the telling, we activate the midbrain, the part of the brain that automatically responds in protective ways to keep us safe, and we may feel triggered or then have a body sensation about something that we had not realized before. We may have a memory that comes floating up from the unconscious that had heretofore been buried.

This memory may be one that we denied and repressed before because it was so disturbing, and we may question if we are imagining something that did not happen. This is the part of talking about what our childhoods were like that is daunting.

When you are remembering trauma in a therapy session, it is never appropriate for the therapist to intervene and try to force you to remember or to tell you whether something is true or not. Your own body does that work. If a memory comes up in therapy and you find yourself doubting its reality, just shelve it for later and trust that if it really happened you will eventually know.

Inside your Self is a very wise person. After the telling of what you actually do know, you may feel exhausted and need to take a break. This is actually recommended, especially if your story is a long one. You can always go back to it later when you are rested.

But you should definitely tell your story because lightness comes at the end, when you are validated and accepted and especially when you hear others tell their stories that are so like your own. You know that you are no longer alone.

Does this mean that you don't remember anymore? No, you will always carry the memories, but after doing your work, you will be the one "driving the bus," rather than your inner child.

Part One:
The Problem

"It is not the bruises on the body that hurt. It is the wounds of the heart and the scars on the mind."

Aisha Mirza

Chapter 1
Who is the Silent Abuser?

We all know abuse when we see or experience it: bruising, hitting with objects, throwing a child across the room, a constant barrage of cursing and hateful comments, abandoning a child on the side of the road, cruelty, and torture. Horrible acts that make us cringe and call for justice. A reason to call Child Protective Services or the police. Children may not realize these acts are abusive when they are children and in the midst of it, but they most certainly can identify this behavior as abuse as adults; that is, if they can remember. Society abhors this sort of behavior and rightly so.

However, there is another abuse that much more difficult to identify. It is silent, yet so painful that it causes people to forget large portions of their childhood in order to survive it. Seldom is this type of abuse reported to a mental health professional at intake. When asked about their family of origin and how it was for them as a child, clients who've suffered this abuse often answer that they had an idyllic childhood with caring parents. They might also say that their parents were good people, but they were unavailable because they were busy with work, volunteer activities, or caring for other family members. Often these clients will add that they can't remember much about their childhood before the age of 12 or 13.

Why the memory lapse? How does this happen?

It happens because the silent abuser was at work. The silent abuser is neglect.

Amalia was the third of four children. She grew up in a small town in the Midwest. As in most small towns, everyone knew everyone else's business. Although it was not spoken about, Amalia knew that appearances were very important.

Her oldest sibling, a sister, was 18 and left home shortly after Amalia was born. Her youngest sibling, a brother, was 3 years younger than herself. Her other sibling, the family's second child, was a boy who was born with a severe disability that rendered him unable to walk, talk, and feed himself.

The family was devastated by this unfortunate circumstance. Amalia's mother carried enormous amounts of shame because, to her, having a child who was not perfect was a reflection on her.

All the family's attention went to the disabled child. Strict rules were established for the rest of the children. Chores were created not to teach the children responsibility, but for doing things the adults could not nor would not do.

In therapy, Amalia could not remember having joy at all as a child. She was virtually ignored except for commands. She was shamed for making poor grades and getting into trouble at school. All the family's energy went into keeping up appearances and caring for her older brother.

Eventually, after Amalia left home to join the military when she was 18, the family placed her disabled brother in a group home. But the damage had been done. Amalia was filled with an anger that she did not understand, alternating with a depression she couldn't shake. When she married, she had trouble regulating her emotions and lashed out at her husband for little things.

Amalia came to therapy for anger issues, which had a negative impact on her marriage. She said, "I feel angry and out of control practically all the time." When asked about her childhood, she talked about how horrible it was for her family and her unfortunate brother who had been so disabled. She also talked about the shame her family felt. However, she did not talk about how it had been for her. Over time, she discovered that the anger she frequently felt was covering all the other feelings that she had had to repress as a child.

After attending an intensive workshop focused on discovering the roots of childhood trauma, Amalia awakened to the fact that she grew up in a rigid, disengaged family that had to focus all its attention on the disabled brother while keeping up appearances in the community. "I had to shut down all my feelings, which were covered over by my anger," she said. "I loved my brother, but I hated that his disability took all the energy away from the rest of us."

Finally, Amalia began a program of Self-care, attending yoga and meditation classes, focusing on what was good about her and letting go of what had gone before. She decided to reduce her contact with her parents and focused on establishing a loving relationship with, first of all, herself, and then her husband and her siblings. A type of therapy known as EMDR (discussed in Chapter 23) helped reduce the emotional impact of the incidents in Amalia's childhood when she was blamed and shamed.

Amalia now has compassion for the angry person that she was. And she embraces her new sense of Self. She visits her disabled brother, now age 57, in the group home as often as she can, and she sees his eyes light up with happiness and recognition when he sees her. She loves and accepts him as he is, and she is able to enjoy the sweetness of the present moment.

Often, parents mistakenly take for granted that the able-bodied children in the family are OK and don't need much if any attention. Just because a child is making good grades, or quiet, or appears to be OK doesn't mean that his or her need for nurturing and attention is any less than that of a disabled child. When a child begins to act out negatively, he or she is often treated as a scapegoat rather than a child silently screaming for the love and attention that he or she so desperately needs and deserves.

Neglect is the cornerstone of all other abuse. It is this foundational wounding that precludes other, more overt types of abuse. What child who experiences overt abuse was valued, loved, seen, accepted and considered?

The degree that a child is neglected ranges from mild to severe. And neglected children sometimes suffer other, more identifiable forms of trauma along with the neglect. As adults, many may seek counseling for addictions, relationship problems, depression, and/or anxiety.

Nevertheless, they still say they had "wonderful parents who exhibited no addictions, were upstanding citizens, attended church, and raised us well." These individuals arrive in therapy not understanding what it is that has caused them to feel such pain.

These clients often exhibit a sunny personality and appear to be successful, and they can't understand why their lives are falling apart. They don't understand they were neglected as children, and that neglect is affecting them as adults.

In clinical terms, neglect is called attachment disorder. Neglect is sometimes used interchangeably with "abandonment." However, the word abandonment brings up images of being physically left, whereas neglect is about people who are physically present but emotionally absent, people who are present but not present at the same time. Neglect feels lonely – extremely lonely – precisely because one is in the presence of others, but the others are not truly there. When one is a child and the "others" are Mommy and Daddy, it can be especially damaging, even life-threatening. The younger a child is when he or she experiences neglect, the more damaging it is.

Chapter 2
Other Forms of Abuse

Physical Abuse: Other kinds of abuse are more overt than neglect. Physical abuse tops the list. Acts of physical abuse are clearly identifiable as abusive. Examples physical abuse include spankings that go on too long, being punished physically when the child has done nothing wrong except to be in the room when the "caregiver" is angry about something else, or drunk or high, throwing things at a child, etc. It is abusive to hit a child when the child is simply being a child by "making too much noise" or asking too many questions. In fact, it is abusive to hit a child for any reason.

Verbal Abuse: Examples of overt verbal abuse include statements about the child's lack of intellectual ability, physical attractiveness, weight, lack of ability to make the parent proud or pleased, and comparing the child to others.

Emotional Abuse: When a child is forbidden to have and express feelings or to have an opinion, that child is being emotionally abused. When a child cannot trust that someone will really hear him/her in a non-judgmental way, that child is being emotionally abused. Controlling a child by telling him/her that frightening things will happen if he or she doesn't "behave" is also an example of emotional abuse.

Another form of emotional abuse involves putting a child into the role of surrogate spouse. This is unfair and abusive, as it forces the child into a role that he/she is not developmentally able to handle. (This is sometimes referred to as "emotional incest" or "covert incest.")

Pushing a child into the role of caregiving the caregiver's emotional needs is also a subtle form of neglect. I say this because the child is not being allowed to just be a child and to naturally develop his or her own sense of self. These children are often identified as a "mommy's boy" or a "daddy's girl" by other family members. It can be hard to recognize this as being traumatic to the child, particularly for a child who thought that he or she was so close to mommy or daddy. But it is definitely abuse, covertly sexual as well as emotional, and the effects are long-lasting.

Sexual Abuse: Usually, when a child experiences **overt** physical or sexual abuse he or she knows it. What applies here are the more subtle forms of sexual abuse. Some of the ways children are sexually violated include voyeurism, failure to give the child adequate privacy, exhibitionism-appearing in front of the child nude or scantily dressed, leering looks, comments about the child's body especially when the child is becoming an adolescent, inappropriate jokes and innuendos. Furthermore, it is emotionally and sexually abusive to ask probing and graphic questions after an older child goes on a date. Lastly, functional parents provide **factual, accurate, non-shaming, and age appropriate** sex education to their children. Remembering that children are innocent and easily shamed, it is important to be available to answer questions, but not force information on the child that they are not yet ready to process.

Many times, as with neglect, men and women do not identify what happened to them as sexual abuse; however, the effects can be long lasting and extreme, resulting in addictive behaviors.

Chapter 3
Spiritual Abuse

The attention to a child's spirit (which is my definition of one's true Self) deserves a chapter of its own, simply because, like neglect, attending to the child's spiritual Self is foundational to healthy development. It plays a huge role in the definition of what it means to be human.

Spiritual abuse includes experiences that distort, retard, or otherwise interfere with a child's spiritual development. Every kind of abuse is spiritual abuse because all forms of abuse wound the soul of the child who experiences it. [1]

When children are small, the parent is the child's Higher Power. Functional parents guide the child to understand that there is a power even greater than them as parents that is loving and nurturing. This doesn't have to be part of an established religion; however, it helps the child to understand that there is a Great Mystery that exists apart from adult humans. Children have deep feelings and are probably more attuned to this than are the parents.

---

1   Mellody, P., Miller, A.W., & Miller, K. (1989). *Facing codependence: What it is, where it comes from, how it sabotages our lives.* Perennial Library.

Dysfunctional parents disempower the child through physical, verbal, emotional, and even sexually abusive behavior, be it overt or covert. Because the child's Higher Power is filtered through the child's view of the parents, anything divine will be seen as rigid, punitive, judgmental, and far, far away. It doesn't feel safe to believe in such a god, because that god is based in fear.

Another form of spiritual abuse occurs when parents falsely empower a child by causing the child to think that he/she is all there is. With this, there are no guidelines or boundaries, and the child is left to believe that he or she ultimately controls everything in his or her life (including parents and other authority figures). Because deep inside the child knows something is off with this belief system, he or she may develop a false persona and act this out in childhood adult life, thus acting as if he or she is the only person that matters and others don't count. We call this "narcissism," and fostering it in a child is a form of spiritual neglect, as it pushes the child away from his or her true Self.

Such false empowering also may lead the child (and later the adult) to believe the delusion that he or she can not only control everything in his or her environment but that he or she can "fix" others whom he or she perceives to be wrong or wounded. The child may achieve success in getting the things and praise that he or she desires from one or both parents. The child may get a teacher or some other authority figure blamed by the parent for the child's misbehavior. Success in influencing the parents like this causes the child to feel powerful when using manipulative tactics and lying. However, this can be problematic in adult life, when others are not so willing to keep the now adult child on his or her self-perceived throne.

You may be thinking, "But wait! Isn't this book about neglect? This falsely empowered child gets loads of attention and support! I don't see that as neglect." Well, it is. Note the word "falsely." The falsely empowered child is still neglected, though in a subtle way. The child is fulfilling some need that the parents have to reflect to others that they have a perfect child who never can make a mistake. Who benefits from this extreme over-permissiveness? Is it the parents (and their reputation) or is it the child?

This is very different from parents who love their child dearly but are also able to teach the child to be accountable and to realize that he or she is human and will make mistakes.

Appropriate teaching and guidance about being accountable to a power greater than oneself is part of parenting and attending to the child's needs. While the child should be able to develop interests based on "who he or she is," the child must also be taught that there is a middle ground between wants and needs. It is appropriate to not only provide for the basic needs of the child, but also the child's wants— but in moderation. Spending quality time with children is sometimes much more meaningful than a new toy or device.

Chapter 4
Addiction to Religion—
A Unique Form of Spiritual Abuse

A common obsession, seldom considered abusive, is when parents are addicted to religion. Pia Mellody outlines characteristics of parents whose religious behaviors may be harmful to children. Ways in which children can be neglected when adult caregivers are addicted to religion include:

1) The concept of God is used as a means to frighten and control the child.

2) Controlling and intimidating by quoting scriptures, particularly ones that start with "Thou shalt not…"

3) Avoiding parental responsibilities by "turning everything over to God." Before you decide that I am suggesting it is not good to turn things over to your Higher Power, listen to this example: I know a rigidly religious couple who locked their 4 and 6-year-old children out of the house for hours while they stayed inside and read their Bible and prayed. When questioned about this, they stated they had "assigned an angel to watch over the kids while they communed with God." Behavior like that is extreme and neglectful.

4) Teaching children that people who have problems are "not right with God."

5) Teaching children that there is only one way to see things. This refers to "them versus us" ideologies. In this philosophy, there always has to be an enemy.

6) Parents who are so busy ministering to the needs of the church and working at the church that they don't give enough time to the needs of their children.

The final example of spiritual/religious neglect/abuse is physical, emotional, or sexual abuse by a religious representative. When a child has no one to turn to and has been taught that God is keeping score, then he or she is more likely to feel shame about what happened, blame him/herself, and suffer in silence. Even parents who are loving and involved with their children may not know or be trusted with something so egregious, but the likelihood of the child trusting the parent enough to share what happened is much greater when parents are present and listening to the feelings and needs of the child.

Debbie's story

Dad had a problem with objectifying women. He also wished Debbie had been a boy so he would have had a son to carry on the family name. Mother was meek and quiet and acquiesced to Dad's directives to be submissive.

Debbie's parents attended a fundamentalist church where she was taught that women were supposed to be silent and submit to their husbands as the head of the household. The family attended church on Sunday mornings, Sunday nights, and Wednesday nights as well as other special services for Bible study and Revivals. Debbie thought the services were boring, but felt afraid of expressing her discontent, because she was taught that God was always watching and would punish her if she disobeyed.

When Debbie was interested in pursuing a medical degree, Dad told her girls are not capable of studying and having careers in the sciences, but perhaps she could be a nurse or an administrative assistant.

When Debbie began to develop into a young woman, Dad made remarks about her changing body. He never directly used sexual words, but he raised his eyebrows and smirked when he saw her coming. Debbie felt ashamed and icky when he did that but didn't quite understand why she felt that way. The family called her a "daddy's girl."

Debbie's mother waited on her father and acquiesced to his every whim. She was given an allowance with which to buy groceries and to buy clothes for the family. She became an expert at learning how to stretch a dollar. She never argued with Dad or said anything when he raged at her or when he laughed at her when she cried.

Debbie learned how wives were to behave by watching her mother. She loved her mother and felt sorry for her.

Because little girls learn about men from watching their fathers, Debbie was attracted to the first boy who paid any attention to her. She also learned to deny her intelligence and her desire to be a physician. She left home to enter into a marriage with Mike at the age of 19. She realized that she wanted to have sex with

Mike but felt it would have been wrong to be sexual outside of marriage.

Debbie's mother modeled for Debbie how women behave in relationships. Debbie swore she would never be like her mother—submissive and being disrespected—yet here she was in a relationship with a man who treated her like her father treated her mother.

It was incredibly painful for Debbie to realize she had become what she disliked most about her mother. She felt empty and unsure of herself and couldn't make decisions about the smallest of things. As a child, others had always made the decisions for her and told her she was wrong if whatever opinion she had differed from theirs. This inability to know what she liked or thought carried over to her relationship with her husband. He made all the decisions.

Debbie ate when she felt anxious and overwhelmed, which was often. When Mike and Debbie discussed having a child, Debbie's doctor told her she would have to lose weight because she had become obese. Debbie tried every diet offered yet was unable to stop eating her feelings. It was only when she began seeing a therapist who specialized in eating disorders that she was able to begin to eat sensibly and to awaken to the fact that she had been thwarted in discovering her own unique Self by her parents and their modeling of a dysfunctional relationship.

Slowly, she learned to eat mindfully and in sync with her appetite. And the weight came off. Mike and Debbie also found a

NEGLECT—THE SILENT ABUSER

church community where they felt welcomed and loved. She learned that she had her own way of seeing the world, and she gave herself permission to discover what she liked and what she thought. It was a revelation to her.

Mike and Debbie worked on their relationship. Actually, Mike was relieved that Debbie had begun to make decisions and have opinions of her own. He welcomed her newfound Self. They learned that the "dance" they did as a couple kept them stuck in the dysfunctional patterns that both of them had modeled for them as children. Mike began to treat Debbie as an equal and to open up to her about his own pain. Debbie learned to state her feelings and needs to Mike. They learned and practiced new ways of relating. Debbie returned to graduate school with plans to enter the medical field.

Four years later, Debbie and Mike had a baby girl, who now will be given the opportunity to grow up in a functional home where she can develop her own sense of Self.

Chapter 5
Why is Neglect Hidden?

The reason I call neglect the hidden abuser is that it is covert. We can't see it, we can't feel it; therefore, we deny it and don't identify it when seeking help. It usually manifests itself as a dark feeling of emptiness inside that nothing can fill. The pain of this emptiness is most often felt either in the chest or in the stomach or both. Those who suffer the pain of neglect may be able to hold it at bay and find many ways to go around it and to dull the pain, but unless it is dealt with and healed, it always comes back.

No parent is perfect. No parent, unless he or she is a sociopath, deliberately harms his or her children. We bring into our adult lives our own childhood wounds. And sometimes we repeat patterns that may have appeared to work for us when we were children (after all, *we* survived), yet these patterns were ultimately not beneficial for us, and they are not beneficial for our children. We are not aware that certain behaviors were harmful to us, and we are not aware that our children need more than what we got.

I am not suggesting that knowing the source of neglectful and abusive behavior by parents in any way excuses it. Ultimately, we are responsible for our behavior, regardless of the reason. I am simply pointing out that patterns tend to repeat, so, without intervention of some sort, neglected children are likely to become neglectful parents.

Chapter 6
High-Risk Families

Neglect is a trauma so subtle that, unless there is overt abuse to go along with it, it is hard to recognize. That said, there are a variety of factors that put children at risk for experiencing neglect. Below I have provided a by no means exhaustive list of examples of situations that may pose a risk for neglect. Please understand that the circumstances leading to neglect vary as much as the complexity of humans and family dynamics themselves.

1) One or both parents suffer from some sort of serious mental illness, and no one talks to the children about it.
2) One or both parents are addicted to alcohol and/or drugs. This risk factor is exacerbated when no one talks to the children about it.
3) One or both parents are workaholics, which signifies that parenting and attentiveness to their children are secondary to their career(s).
4) Economic conditions dictate that the parents work more than one job, leaving no time/energy for parenting the children.
5) One or more siblings are sick, troubled, needy, or handicapped and require attention that the other children do not get.

6) A sibling is talented in one area and the parents choose to focus on the achievements of that child to the detriment of the other children.

7) There is infidelity and/or sexual addiction on the part of one parent, which causes the other parent to become so overcome with the devastation that no time or energy is left for the children.

8) In a single parent household, the parent is more focused on finding and keeping a good mate than on caring for the child(ren).

9) One parent dies or leaves the family, leaving the other parent grief-stricken and unable to be there to attend to the grief of (and other needs of) the children.

10) When the birth of a child is unexpected or unwanted. Most people are thrilled to learn they will become new parents. Some pregnancies, however, happen unexpectedly or at an inopportune time in the life of the parent. There may be conflict, infidelity, addiction, even violence in the relationship between the mother and father of the baby. There may not be enough money to raise a child. The list of reasons for unwanted pregnancies goes on and on, and any reason is a risk factor for neglect.

Felicity was given the task of caring for her younger brother and sister when she was growing up. She took her responsibility of being a 5-year-old caregiver very seriously. She changed her sister's diapers, made sure she didn't get into trouble, and climbed up on the kitchen chair to make hot dogs for her younger siblings. She accompanied her brother and sister everywhere they went. When her sister, Maria, fell off her bike and broke her arm, Felicity blamed herself for not watching Maria more closely.

Felicity's brother and sister doted on her and looked upon her as a mother figure. Her brother, Mike, got into drugs and alcohol as a teenager and eventually overdosed, thus ending his life. Maria married and moved away. Felicity was devastated by both of these events.

You might be wondering, "Where were Felicity's parents?" They were both high functioning alcoholics who loved to socialize. Mother hid her drinking well but was deeply depressed. Mother's drinking and depression were untreated throughout Felicity's childhood. Father, in addition to drinking, had serial affairs with women who worked for him. The parents stayed together because of their religious beliefs and to maintain their public image.

Felicity married a man who was addicted to gambling. The occasional gambling had started small, but gradually morphed into something that was stealing the family's savings.

When Felicity entered therapy, it was to address the desperation she was feeling over her husband's gambling. She felt she had tried everything to get him to stop, but nothing worked. Felicity was in crisis. The therapist gently helped Felicity validate her heroic efforts to help her husband. She did not label nor shame her for how she was coping with this distressing situation. Felicity was able to find a balance between loving and caring for her family while, at the same time, affirming and caring for herself. The question, "What about you?" continued to be brought up in therapy. "What do you want, what do you feel?" This was a revelation to Felicity – this mindful focus on herself. Felicity began to get in touch with her total lack of Self-knowledge. She

*had been programmed to be the little adult who took care of oth-
ers' needs and wants, rather than having thoughts, feelings, and
needs of her own. While it was natural and loving to try to repair
the damage being done to her husband and the family by this
addiction, Felicity had difficulty balancing the need to support
him with the need to take care of herself.*

*Over time, Felicity initially discovered a wellspring of repressed
resentment and crippling sadness for the neglect that she had suffered as a child. Eventually, she learned not only that it is impossible
to fix others but that expecting a child to be a primary caregiver
to younger siblings is abusive and neglectful. She found that an
inward journey was necessary to find her undiscovered Self.*

Felicity's story is a variation of a theme that I hear quite often. This
theme describes a childhood in which one child takes on the responsibility of playing the role of the parent to younger siblings or acting
as the caregiver to Mom or Dad. All the energy of the child goes outward to others, thus denying the child's own needs.

Why does this happen? The answer varies from the death of one
parent, a divorce, addicted parents, mental illness, a general lack of
parenting and neglect of the children. The results are children (now
adults) who are vulnerable and whose lives are never fully realized
until they get help. This is heartbreaking.

Chapter 7
The Other Side of Neglect— Too Much Control

Horatio is 8 years old. Horatio wishes he were bigger so he could protect Mommy. Daddy's always mad when he is home. Daddy has to work a lot. When he is home, Daddy and Mommy yell and scream at each other. Horatio hides in the closet and distracts himself by playing with the shoes. He hates himself for being a coward.

Horatio loves and fears his dad, and feels special when he is gone. This is when Mom looks at Horatio and talks to him about her problems and about other grown-up stuff. She tells Horatio that she doesn't know what she would do without him. She says she loves to spend time with him, sharing her deepest thoughts and feelings, discussing ideas, confiding in him, telling him her sorrows about how Dad has done her wrong.

Unconsciously, Mom wants little Horatio to be there for her in ways that his dad is not. She has no idea of the damage she is doing to him by making him her surrogate spouse. Little Horatio loves his mother and wants her to be happy, so he complies, And inside he takes on the huge responsibility for her happiness while secretly (and unconsciously) resenting her.

Years later, as an adult, Horatio can't understand why he feels resentful toward his mother sometimes, so he also feels guilty for resenting her. In addition, as hard as he has always tried to please his mother, she continues to be unhappy. Horatio internalizes her pain, taking it on as his own. He doesn't realize that the idea that a child can possibly "fix" a parent is and always has been totally unrealistic.

Unfortunately for Horatio, little boys first learn about what women are like from watching their mothers. What do you think Horatio learned? From his mother he learned that women are needy and unhappy and overbearing.

Horatio also watched his father when he was home. He learned from his father to hide his feelings, to openly express anger, and to disrespect women as weak and lesser than men. Horatio's parents lacked an intimate relationship, primarily because his father was unavailable. His mother was hurting and unable to get through to his father.

When Horatio started dating, Mom felt that there was no one who measured up to her son. She criticized each girlfriend so much that Horatio began keeping secrets about his interest in anyone. Mom wanted to know each and every detail about every girl he dated. So he put off having a serious girlfriend until he started college.

Mom wanted a university in the same city so Horatio could stay home while attending classes. Horatio, in a valiant attempt to escape, chose an out of state university and was accepted there. Once there, he went wild. He had many one-night stands and short relationships, kicking each girl to the curb whenever he began having feelings for her beyond the excitement of the sexual encounter.

In his senior year of college, Horatio met a girl, Gladys, who was intelligent and beautiful. They became good friends. She shared with him about her mother, who was an active alcoholic, and her father, who worked all the time. Horatio loved her. It made him feel important to help her and to listen to her troubles. Soon they made plans to become engaged and eventually to marry.

Horatio dreaded the meeting with the parents. But Gladys's parents were open and welcoming. They loved to party and have fun, and Horatio couldn't understand why Gladys had made such a big deal about her mother's drinking. They were fun. He thought, "They're better than my mother and father, who are sad and boring and seem to hate one another."

When he finally took Gladys home to meet his parents, they, too, were happy for him. His dad, especially, was kind and welcoming to Gladys. His mother, however, though polite, cried and told Horatio in private that she needed him to move back home. When they went out to dinner to celebrate the engagement, his mother lost her purse and much of the evening was spent in the drama of searching for the purse. Gladys told Horatio later that she thought his mother didn't like her, which Horatio, though he knew it to be true.

Horatio's mother's behavior became a pattern that continued into his marriage and the birth of his children, with Mom continually creating drama and bringing attention to herself. Horatio handled the strain by telling himself that "he needed a drink." Eventually, his drinking increased to the point where Gladys concluded that she needed help for herself. She started therapy and began attending meetings for Al-Anon and Adult Children of Alcoholics (ACoA). To her great dismay, Gladys realized she had married an alcoholic, and after 10 years of marriage she decided to leave the relationship.

Gladys filed for divorce. Horatio, whose drinking had increased to the point that he'd lost his job, moved home with his mother. He was devastated and angry that Gladys had left him, so to numb the pain of it, he drank even more. His father had passed away, and Horatio didn't know what else to do but move back in with his mother to "take care of her."

This is an unfortunate ending to an all-too-common story. The good news is that many neglected and overcontrolled people are able to reach out for help and become conscious of the fact that they were manipulated as children to be their parent(s) caregivers. They work through the resultant anger and sadness and are able to set appropriate boundaries with Mom and/or Dad and to discover who they really are and what they really want in life while still treating their parents with respect. Sadly, Horatio was in so much in pain and denial that he could not do so.

Being overly controlling of everything children think, feel, and do is a form of neglect. Children in controlling families get loads of attention, but it has a negative quality to it. The practice of controlling every thought or feeling a child naturally has only satisfies the needs of the parents. It does not help the child do his or her own thinking. Rather than being guided and heard for his or her own sake, the child is forced into a box of the parents' making. The child is not allowed to discover his or her own sense of Self and what his or her own likes and dislikes are. I call this "neglect of the soul."

What happens to overly controlled children? First of all, they feel overwhelmed. They begin to think their own feelings and thoughts are wrong and they defer to whatever the adult caregiver says. They learn to not think for themselves. Instead, they become dependent on what somebody else says, or they learn to lie and cover up how they really feel. Having given up who they are as individuals, they eventually feel empty and unable to access their feelings.

Children come into this world with needs, starting with basic survival. They need to be fed, cleaned, attended to, and loved. At each stage of development, guidance directed at teaching life skills to the child is needed. In an ideal situation, the energy goes in the direction of the child, not the other way around. Keeping in mind that the child will grow up and will need skills to operate in this world independently, the parents' teachings build on themselves as the child matures. But when the child is over-controlled by the parents, the child does not adequately develop these much-needed skills.

Part Two: Brain Matters

"The Body Keeps the Score"

Bessel A. van der Kolk

Chapter 8
Trauma is Stored in the Brain

The next few chapters discuss research that traces where neglect and the effects of neglect come from. This chapter is on attachment disorder—the set of symptoms that describes the results of neglect in childhood. I have tried to make the wording as user-friendly as possible, and to keep the discussion brief. After all, you're not studying to do brain surgery, you're just trying to find your Self. That said, I think you will find this information about the brain fascinating.

Generally speaking, attachment disorder manifests as a vague feeling of emptiness inside. John Bradshaw calls it "the hole in the soul." There often is a feeling of not belonging, of being separate from others, of not being "enough."

The process of dealing with this is painful. Therefore, the child will seek external substances and/or behaviors to dull the pain and not feel. Eventually, especially in adolescence and adulthood, the "emotional escape" processes that worked in childhood can start to cause more harm than good. This is especially true when coping mechanisms become addictions. In time, feelings of abandonment and despair are so deeply repressed that the adult cannot remember many details of his or her childhood, or, if the adult does remember, no emotions accompany the memories.

In the 1950s and 60s, Dr. John Bowlby was the first to publish papers on attachment theory. A basic outline of his theory was set forth in three papers: "The Nature of the Child's Tie to His Mother" (1958)[2]; "Separation Anxiety" (1959)[3]; and "Grief and Mourning in Infancy and Early Childhood" (1960)[4]. As with any new theory, Bowlby's ideas were initially controversial, but over time they have proven to be true.

Essentially, what Bowlby found is that everything that happens to us from the womb to the tomb is stored in the body. Even before birth, the mood and emotions of the mother can affect the child. When a mother is stressed, the adrenal glands produce cortisol, which then passes through the placenta to the unborn baby. The influx of cortisol has been shown to have effects on the child's development both pre and post-birth.

We needn't consciously remember the effects of neglect or abuse to feel its effects. In fact, we often don't remember. This is because our bodies have marvelous built-in mechanisms for survival. They do not allow us to consciously remember trauma until we are strong enough to do so. Memories of trauma stay stuck in the nether regions of the brain which are not accessible by the frontal lobes-- the thinking, conscious part of the brain.

Do you ever overreact or feel weird about a situation without understanding why you feel so upset or abandoned or out of control? If so, it's likely that you have called up a feeling from the unconscious part

---

2   Bowlby, J. (1958). The nature of the child's tie to his mother. *International journal of psycho-analysis, 39, 350-373.*

3   Bowlby, J. (1960). Separation anxiety. *The international journal of psycho-analysis, 41, 89-113.*

4   Bowlby, J., (1960). Grief and Mourning in Infancy and Early Childhood. *The psychoanalytic study of the child, 15(1), 9-52.*

of your brain because the present situation is similar in some way to a traumatic situation in your past. The current situation has unconsciously triggered a reaction to past trauma.

Chapter 9
Parts of the Brain

The human brain is extremely complex and fascinating. Weighing approximately 3 pounds, it contains approximately 100 billion neurons and 100 trillion connections, all working together. It is constantly reorganizing itself and adaptable to change. Current research shows us that the brain can heal and rewire itself in response to injury. It is truly a magnificent creation. To understand ourselves, I believe it is important to have a rudimentary understanding of how the brain works.

Because most of you are not students of brain chemistry, I have included a simple diagram of the major parts of the human brain and some of the responsibilities of each part. In looking at the duties of each part we can better understand why much of our knowledge of ourselves and why we act and feel the way we do, is not clear to our conscious minds. Please pay particular attention to the parts of the temporal lobe, which is part of the limbic system. I have printed these parts in bold. This area is where our unconscious memories and emotions are stored, and it is from these parts (especially the amygdala) that we get triggered.

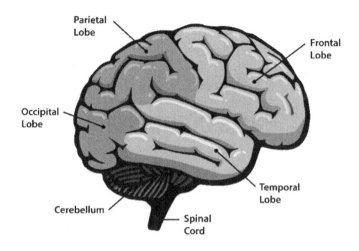

Parts of the Human Brain

- Spinal Cord/Brain stem [unconscious]: oversees internal milieu of body (autonomic functions) by regulating temperature, heart rate, basic reflexes, arousal, and pain systems.
- **Cerebellum [unconscious]: coordinates and regulates muscular activity (fight, flight, or freeze)**
- **Temporal Lobe which is part of the Limbic System [unconscious]: This is the part of the brain that is involved with emotion, learning, memory, and mediation of primitive approach/avoidance responses and the area of motivation. Moreover, it is where autonomic cues are received from the body. For our purpose here, important parts to know are:**
  * Pituitary gland-located in the limbic system but actually part of the endocrine system. Called the master gland because it performs so many tasks. Its main function is to secrete hormones into the bloodstream.

***Hypothalamus-responsible for motivation of hunger and thirst; regulation of body temperature; controls release of hormones by the pituitary gland.**

***Amygdala-stores responses and memory of emotions, <u>especially of fear.</u>**

***Hippocampus-processing of long-term memory and emotional responses.**

- Occipital Lobe [unconscious]: Visual processing center
- Parietal Lobe [unconscious]: processes sensory information regarding location of parts of the body as well as interpreting visual information and processing language and mathematics.
- Frontal Lobe [conscious]: responsible for motor function, problem solving, decision making, language, judgment, impulse control and social behavior
- The Cerebral Cortex (not pictured on this diagram): the large portion of folded gray matter covering the outer portion of the brain. It plays a key role in memory, attention, perception, cognition, awareness, thought, language, and consciousness.

LEFT BRAIN-RIGHT BRAIN AND BRAIN WAVES

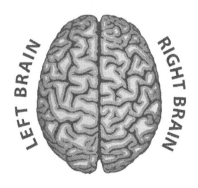

In addition, the human brain has two hemispheres (left and right) separated by a network of nerve fibers called the corpus callosum. The corpus callosum is the largest collection of white matter within the brain, and it has a high myelin content. Myelin is a fatty, protective coating around nerves that facilitates quicker transmission of information. (Source: Healthline.com)

The left brain is responsible for linear and analytical thought. It performs tasks that have to do with logic such as science and mathematics. The right brain is responsible for emotions, creativity and artistic endeavors. Both sides and all parts of the brain work together; however, one or the other side tends to be dominant. It is believed that EMDR (or bilateral stimulation) allows both sides of the brain to communicate across the corpus callosum; therefore, bringing unconscious information/feelings to the surface and reducing the impact of emotional trauma. We don't understand exactly how and why this works; we only know that it does.

The right brain of the cerebral cortex develops in the first stages of life (birth to about age 2). This is the time when mothers mirror emotions to their infants by interacting with them face to face. The baby learns through observing and taking in information provided by his or her primary caregiver (usually the mother). If the caregiver is chronically unavailable or chronically angry and stressed out, the baby will take that in. I say chronically because no caregiver can be available and on an even keel 100% of the time.

Over time, the baby learns that his or her mother will return when she goes away. She can be trusted to be there when the baby needs her. This is not to put a guilt trip on mothers who work and leave the baby with another caregiver. The important thing to remember is babies need time, care, and attention from one to three caregivers during infancy. With this, the baby will learn to recognize and trust. Without it, not so much.

Moreover, brain waves come online in a sequence based on age to match the development of the child. Delta waves, the lowest activity of brain function, come online in the neonatal (infancy) stage. Theta waves are most prominent from ages 2 to 6 when children are downloading information from their environment into their subconscious.

This is the age of imaginary play, when children begin to mix play with reality, and theta waves play an important role in this. Alpha waves, which come online about age 6, use both sides of the brain at the same time. This is the time that children become more focused and alert with ideas and inspiration, though still able to be peaceful and relaxed as well. Beta waves come online about age 12, when the focus is on consciousness in the schoolroom.[5]

Notice in the following story how Linda used her theta waves to go into a trance, which helped her to cope:

Linda

Linda was the baby of the family and the only girl. She had 3 brothers who were almost grown when she was born. Her parents often called her by the nickname, "Oopsie," because they thought they were through having children when she came along.

Linda says her first memories are of her parents arguing when she was about 4-5 years old. There were violent confrontations between her parents, and between her father and an older brother who was about 16 at the time.

Nevertheless, Linda's family was respected, financially stable, involved in community activities, and socially connected. Linda's

---

5   Lipton, B. H. (2008). "Learning and Brain States." In Lipton, B., *The wisdom of your cells: How your beliefs control your biology* [Audiobook: disk 6, track 6]. Sounds True.
Lipton, B. H. (2005) *The biology of belief: Unleashing the power of consciousness, matter and miracles.* Authors Pub Corp.

father owned his own business and worked long hours. Mother was a stay at home parent who volunteered in many organizations and was focused on her appearance and how her children looked and behaved. She was a strict believer in the saying, "Children should be seen and not heard." The family rule, spoken or unspoken, was "don't talk, don't feel, and never tell anyone anything about what goes on in this family."

*Linda appeared to her family to be slow in her development. She was very quiet and shy. Mostly, she stayed in her room and read. School was an escape from the fighting. **The adults thought she was "slow" because she stared into space and daydreamed a lot.***

In spite of what her parents assumed, Linda did well in school and graduated college. School had always given her relief from the negative energy of her home, and she thrived in an academic environment away from her family.

When Linda came to therapy for severe depression, she didn't understand why she couldn't just pull out of it. In her adult life, she seemed to quickly and easily be drawn into relationships with men who were emotionally unavailable and could not be faithful to her. The last one duped her out of her life savings.

Through therapy, Linda learned that hearing the words that she was a mistake (even though it was veiled as a family joke) convinced her that she was flawed and did not deserve to be treated well. She blamed herself (as children often do) when there was conflict in her family. As an adult, she repeated the pattern of not expecting much from her relationships, thinking, albeit on an unconscious level, that she needed to change herself to suit her partner.

Linda began to understand that what she experienced as a child set her up for choosing people who would not be emotionally available for her. She began to set boundaries for herself and to listen to her inner guidance system. In the process, she got to know someone she had never paid much attention to – herself. Moreover, she learned to accept and honor that Self. As she became more empowered, she began to attract people who were honest and respectful.

Linda's story is an example of the subtle neglect that occurs when a child is unexpected and is born into a family that is more focused on how it looks to outsiders than on the needs of the people within it. This is confusing for children; what they are told is the truth of their family is incongruent with what they actually see. Layered onto this confusion is the fact that they are forbidden to speak or ask about the disconnect between what they are told and the reality of what they experience.

Chapter 10
The Role of Genes and Epigenetics

Current research looking at addictions is exciting and revolutionary. We are coming to understand that the underlying causes of dysfunctional human behavior, the inability to regulate emotions, addictive behaviors, and other behavioral issues can be traced to human development and thus gene development throughout generations of dysfunctional family perceptions.

When we understand that the way we think, feel, and behave is related to unconscious *acquired* perceptions in the cells of our body, we can pinpoint what is going on with our feelings and behaviors and where our inabilities to control ourselves come from. Have you ever sworn to yourself that you will never behave like your father or mother, and then you find yourself saying and doing the exact things you promised yourself you would never say and do? If so, an understanding of epigenetics can help you to not be so hard on yourself and to be mindful of what is happening. When you understand where your unwanted thoughts come from, you can begin to make changes in your perceptions and thinking.

The word "epigenetics" simply means "above the genes." What this means is there are heritable (changes in gene function that are not involved in the DNA sequence. The way we see, believe, and react to the world around us is acquired based on the how our ancestors and, most strongly, our parents see, believe, and react to their own environment. These "acquired perceptions" from generations back can affect tendencies for certain diseases, as well as emotional development and patterns of behavior.[6]

Simply stated, epigenetics influence our behavior. Research is finding that ways of experiencing the world can be passed down from generation to generation until or unless that way of thinking and way of behaving is recognized and changed. The first line of defense is the recognition. The human body is marvelously adaptable as a way of ensuring our survival. Therefore, as discussed in the previous chapter, our inner psyche provides a wide array of ways in which we can avoid feeling the enormous pain of a neglectful or abusive reality.

Children learn more by observation than by what parents say. So, although someone may not be able to recall hearing their family actually say a certain thing, the child felt the energy of those (spoken or unspoken) words, and that developed a certain belief. Children observe their parents' moods, facial expressions, tone of voice, cause and effect, sighs, and a host of other non-verbal cues that speak volumes. The following example shows how childhood experiences may unconsciously affect adult feelings and behavior.

Tammy had trouble sitting at the dinner table with her husband and children. She hated to cook, but even when she ordered take-out, she hated to sit down with her family to eat it. In therapy, Tammy talked about how her body became rigid and her

---

6   Lipton, B. H. (2008). *The wisdom of your cells: How your beliefs control your biology* [Audiobook, disc 6]. Sounds True.

shoulders felt tight and her throat constricted whenever it was time to sit down at the table. When asked by the therapist what dinner time was like in her family of origin, Tammy recalled that the expectation was that all the family eat together. Her mother, dad, older brother, and younger sister were at the table as well. Dad was from a military background. He said the same grace every night. Then the family was subjected to a steady barrage of negative political rhetoric from Dad. Tammy remembered that her mother's face became fixed and rigid when Dad began talking and that she obediently nodded her head as they ate. Once, her brother offered a differing opinion from Dad, but Dad put him in his place immediately by rapping him on the head with the handle of his knife. As Tammy shared this story, her body became rigid and her face fixed. She had learned at the childhood dinner table to shut down her body and keep her mouth shut, shutting out any opinion of her own. She had also learned to avoid her feelings. Her psyche was at work to help her survive. But now, as an adult, this coping mechanism was no longer working.

Another factor to consider is that neglected and abused children growing up in dysfunctional homes experience chaos in their surroundings. From age 0-6, whatever the child experiences is downloaded into the subconscious mind. The subconscious mind is habitual, meaning it will play out the program of childhood until the adult changes it.

Furthermore, chaotic homes create continual stress. In the body, the hypothalamus, pituitary, and adrenal glands secrete chemicals meant to help the human survive immediate danger. This is called activation of the HPA axis. When the HPA axis is activated, blood flow is directed less to the frontal lobes of the brain (the thinking and reasoning portion of the brain) and more to the hind-brain (the automatic-response "fight, flight, or freeze" portion of the brain). [7]

When blood flow to the part of the brain that handles reasoning and decision making is constricted, we are not able to make wise decisions about our behavior. Neglected and otherwise abused people can get accustomed to that chaotic state of high arousal, and they find that they are not able to react appropriately or execute good judgment in triggering circumstances. In the example above, this is seen in Tammy's inability to sit comfortably at the dinner table with her family. Fortunately, research is finding that the brain can develop new pathways leading to new behaviors in adults.

---

7   Lipton, B. H. (2008). "The HPA Axis." In Lipton, B., *The wisdom of your cells: How your beliefs control your biology* [Audiobook disc 5, track 8]. Sounds True.

Part Three: Healing

"In life one plays the hand one is dealt to the best of one's ability. Those who insist on playing, not the hand they were given, but the one they insist they should have been dealt—these are life's failures. We are not asked if we will play. That is not an option. Play we must. The option is how."

Anthony de Mello

In my years of practicing psychotherapy, there is one single thing that saddens me the most—the loss of potential. I imagine what life could have been like for all the children who were born with all the raw material they needed for an abundant life. Yet, because of the inability and dysfunction of the family into which they were born, they were denied the opportunities they needed to achieve lasting happiness and wholeness. And there are other contributing factors, apart from the family, that can influence and block the potential of humans to become fully who they were meant to be. Economic instability, predators outside the family of origin, the negative influence of poor teachers, preachers who don't know what they are doing, trauma from war, jobs that require inhumane hours, political barriers, and social barriers based on race, gender, sexual orientation, etc., just to name a few. Unforeseen accidents and illnesses also are contributing factors.

Nevertheless, I can't help but believe that in spite of life's ups and downs people can overcome their past and thrive.

Still, is it helpful to find and assign blame? I think not. Admittedly, it is important for struggling adults to wake up to the realities of what happened to them in childhood, and to have a clear understanding of how they suffered and how that limited their ability to develop to their full potential. But after getting in touch with the truth of their former lives, they must face forward and live in the present, because the past is forever gone.

Now they must do the work of healing. The path is set before them, and it is not an easy path. It truly is a hero's journey. The choice to embark or not embark upon this trek is theirs to make.

Chapter 11
The Decision to Change

Rufus was born to parents who married in their thirties. This was the second marriage for both of them. They had no children in their previous marriages, choosing instead to focus on their careers. Neither of them even imagined that they would want children. That is, until Rufus' mom hit 40. Then she realized how desperately she wanted a child, as did Rufus' dad.

When Mom became pregnant right away after stopping birth control, they were both ecstatic. Several months into the pregnancy, they found out it was a boy. Dad envisioned a big burly son who would be a football player like himself. In fact, Dad brought a child-sized football to the hospital delivery room when Rufus was born.

However, Rufus was small like his mother, and shy as a small child. He couldn't seem to get the hang of throwing the football and was more interested in music. He excelled in school in music and academia.

Rufus was not what Dad had imagined he would be, and Dad was not happy about it. When Dad took Rufus deer hunting at age 10 and Rufus shot one (to please his dad), Rufus cried. He told his dad he never wanted to have anything to do with guns again. Instead he wanted a piano. Dad was furious and forbid it. Rufus was not going to be allowed to do anything "sissy" like that.

When Rufus confided to his mother that he thought he was gay, she was loving and kind and told him not to tell his father, because, according to Mother, "it would kill him." Rufus already knew not to do that. When Rufus was 16 he had many friends who were girls, but no girlfriends, and he didn't seem to be interested in dating. Father noticed and confided to Rufus' mother in a sarcastic way that he was worried about Rufus. When Mother suggested that perhaps Rufus was gay, Father scoffed and laughed, remarking, "Not my boy! Never!"

Consequently, Rufus kept this reality about himself hidden, but inside he felt broken and flawed. He paid careful attention to how he walked and talked, not wanting to appear different or to ever be called "gay." He dated girls, even though he was not sexually attracted to them. Girls loved him. He didn't make advances and was friendly and fun on a date. He listened to their problems; he was their friend. In this way, Rufus could keep his father thinking that because he had lots of "girlfriends," he really must be heterosexual after all.

One girl with whom he was friends had an older brother who was also his friend. Rufus fell in love with him. When on a camping trip one summer after Rufus was in college, he confessed his feelings to the brother, the brother's reaction was to become enraged and then to laugh at Rufus. The other boy then told his mother, and she called Rufus' mother. It was the worst day of Rufus' life. His heart had been broken, he couldn't change his feelings, and the desperate hopelessness he felt lead to depression.

Rufus saw a psychiatrist for medication to alleviate his depression, but this did not alleviate the pain of being gay in a society that would not accept him, and especially the pain of being rejected by his father. So he hid his pain and moved to a big city where no one knew him. He went online, solicited anonymous sex with men, and frequented bathhouses and bookstores. At first, it felt exciting to be validated in this way. But having lots of sex wasn't enough to cover his Self-loathing. Eventually, he started using poppers and then cocaine.

After a while, Rufus grew tired of the constant partying and met someone online with whom he fell in love. There was only one problem. His newfound love, Bill, refused to tolerate his drug use and constant hookups. Rufus knew he had to decide what was more important.

He'd had a glimpse of what life could really be like without the artificial excitement of casual sex and drug use and the shame he felt afterward, so he joined a gay-friendly 12-step group and got sober from cocaine. It was the hardest thing he ever did until he also entered recovery for his sexual addiction. His partner was long-suffering and patient with all of this.

When Rufus achieved a year of sobriety from all his addictions, he entered therapy to deal with his now-estranged parents. He came to the place of accepting that no matter what his father and mother said or did, he was going to be all right. He was out and proud and no longer had anything of which to be ashamed.

He and Bill got married. Only his close newfound family attended. His parents refused to come. The end of this story is that Rufus will forever carry sadness for his parents' refusal to accept him, but he also can feel the joy of being who he really was meant to be. He found the true Self that had been denied him as a child.

What do you do if you resonate with some (or all) of what I've written so far?

I believe, first and foremost, that it is important to decide if you want to do something about it. You may be blown away by the idea that something was amiss in your childhood that's affecting your life today. You might notice problems in your intimate relationship, your relationships with others (family members, coworkers, friends, strangers, other drivers on the road, what you perceive as God, etc.), and even the way you react to current events.

If you have experienced neglect, it is likely that you have learned to shut down your feelings in order to survive. Your psyche has very wisely developed a mechanism to allow you to function on the outside, even though something may be very wrong and well hidden inside. Through distracting yourself with staying busy or obsessing about things on the outside, you may not even be aware of the pain you carry on the inside.

Once you stop distracting yourself, you will begin to get in touch with your own woundedness. Although feeling the pain hurts, it allows you to connect with your emotions and attach a name to what you feel. This is a necessary step in Self-realization. With this realization, you recognize that the mechanism that got you through to your adult life is no longer serving you well or at all. It is time to change.

This change takes time, commitment, and great courage. Are you up for it?

Why, you might ask, should I bother to go through the pain involved in getting in touch with my emotions? What's the point of changing? To quote Father Richard Rohr, "As we go through life, the hurts, disappointments, betrayals, abandonments, and the burden of our sinfulness [imperfections] and brokenness pile up and we do not know what to do with it all. *If we do not transform this pain, we will most assuredly transmit it, usually to those closest to us: our family, our neighbors, our work partners, and, invariably, the most vulnerable, our children.*" [italics mine]

Remember that everything changes. Through doing the work of feeling and healing, you will find that your life *does* improve, and the pain you (re)experience will not have the same degree of emotional impact on you as it did before. Most importantly, you will break the chain for future generations. That's an awesome legacy!

If you have decided that you would like to make a change, I have provided some basic realizations and recommendations in the chapters that follow. You may have never considered these ideas before because all of us tend to be incredibly distracted by coping with all that goes on in our lives and in the world. So, get ready to be challenged. I would ask that if you read something that sounds preposterous and/ or confusing you neither accept nor reject it. Instead, just sit in silence with the idea and consider it.

Chapter 12
Who Are You Really?

Most people operate from their unconscious mind a good percentage of the time. Think of your conscious mind as being like an iceberg. All that you can see is above the water. However, most of the iceberg (usually around 90%) is hidden beneath the water, where it cannot easily be seen.

As was discussed in Part 2, on how the brain operates and affects us, the unconscious mind has a huge influence on how we think and feel, even though we don't realize it. Therefore, in order to know what we are dealing with and to drop the survival mechanisms that were formed when we were a child, we have to *go within* to find out what these survival mechanisms are. It is only when we know ourselves in this way that we can be awake and aware enough to do something about it.

In her book, *The Spiritual Dimension of the Enneagram,* Sandra Maitri speaks of Essence, our essential nature by discussing the Enneagram. The Enneagram is a practice based on nine psychological personality types.

To quote Maitri:

"The process of losing contact with our essential nature is universal: everyone who develops an ego goes through it. Point Nine on the

Enneagram represents the fundamental principle that initiates ego development: the actual loss of our True Nature. This loss of contact is often referred to in spiritual work as falling asleep, resulting in a state of ignorance or darkness. The process of losing contact with that which is innate and unconditioned occurs gradually during the first few years of life, and by the time we are four years old, Essence is mostly lost to perception. This loss of consciousness of our essential nature starts the development of the scaffolding that is the ego structure.

Developing this structure is a necessary prerequisite for spiritual development, since part of the ego's attainment is Self-reflective consciousness. Without it, we could not be aware of our own consciousness. Ultimately, [why this takes place] remains a mystery, and our beliefs about the purpose behind this loss are immaterial. It is simply a given, and we can either deal with our estrangement or remain asleep to it."[8]

Heretofore, I have quoted material that deals the universal development of all humans. For our purposes here, I would like to skip to the factors involved in ego development that are related to abuse and neglect. Inadequate attentiveness to an infant's needs (neglect) naturally causes the baby to cry in an attempt to relieve his or her pain from whatever need is not being met by the caregiver. As the child experiences more and more loss of attention and responsiveness, his or her energy will be focused on reacting to an environment that cannot be trusted to meet his or her survival needs. The child develops strategies to deal with a world that is not to be trusted, and as he or she internalizes these beliefs about the environment he or she is growing up in, he or she begins to apply these beliefs to the rest of the outside world. These are the beliefs that shape the child's (and later the adult's) ego.

---

8   Maitri, S. (2000). *The spiritual dimension of the enneagram: Nine faces of the soul* (pp. 27-28). Penguin.

If parents are not capable of perceiving, valuing, and tuning in to who *they* really are, then they cannot and will not pass that ability on to their children by mirroring a healthy sense of Self. Often, after being continually neglected, children begin to wonder what there is about them that is so flawed that their parent(s) don't connect with them. So, in essence, they blame themselves for the neglect they experience.

Another factor that suggests that epigenetics (influences "above the genes") play a role in the ways of being and thinking that children develop is how they, in early infancy, develop perceptions based on the perceptions of the mother. For the first few months of life, infants fail to recognize that they are a discrete person apart from their mother.

Since our consciousness during these crucial months is merged with that of our mother, what she experiences of us becomes what we experience of ourselves. In other words, as infants we become what our mother perceives us to be. In this way, our parents' society, culture, and worldview are passed on to us.

Chapter 13
What Does it Mean to
Know Your Self?

Florence's story

Some parents try for years to conceive and then, for whatever reason, are cautioned to only have one baby. When that child is finally born, all the hopes and dreams of the parents are placed on this one child. Florence was just such a "miracle child."

Florence's mother had childhood onset diabetes and was not supposed to have children. Nevertheless, her sisters were having large families—one sister had 5 children and another had 6— and Florence Sr. and her husband Jack wanted a child of their own. They made the decision to go to a fertility specialist and, in time, little Florence was born.

Florence was named after her mother because the rule in their family was that the eldest child is named after her parent. Thus, the name Florence, even though her mother also hated the name.

Mother had risked her life to have the baby. Florence was subtly reminded of this fact by being called the "million-dollar baby" and the "miracle baby." From the time she was conceived, her life had been strategically planned. Subconsciously, she knew her purpose in life was to make her parents happy. Florence was closely and carefully monitored to make sure she thought, felt, and acted as her parents wanted. When she expressed a differing thought, she was interrupted by her father and told, "Oh no, no, no, no, that's not right," and, "Here is the way you should think," and, "You shouldn't feel that way."

Mother now felt that she had kept up with her sisters by having a child, even though her health was fragile, and she relished staying home and being a mom. While Dad was at work, Mother made Florence into a living, breathing doll. She cut and styled her hair, picked out her clothes, and chose her friends by inviting little girls over whom Florence didn't particularly like. In fact, Florence was forbidden from having anything to do with many of the children that she liked because her parents disapproved of them. And these were not children who were a bad influence; they were a little girl whose mother was divorced, and another girl whose family was from the North and openly confronted racism.

As Florence approached puberty, Mother and Father focused on helping Florence "find a good man to take care of her" rather than becoming educated and independent. Florence was a smart child but quickly learned that being intelligent was not honored in girls, even though she was still expected to make As and Bs. It was expected that she would attend college, but only to receive a limited education while searching for "the right man."

When Florence was an adolescent, her mother died from cancer. During the summer of her 13th year, her father chose to return to work and leave his dying, bedridden wife home alone with Florence. Their neighbor, who was a nurse, came over at regular intervals to give Florence's mother shots of morphine. In July, her mother died. This was the event that completed her sense of despair and emptiness.

On the day after her mother's funeral, Florence was molested by her uncle, who was entrusted to babysit her while her father returned to work. She told no one, feeling ashamed and embarrassed. On a later occasion, this same uncle grabbed her thigh in the car in front of her father. No one paid any attention. Florence knew at this point that it would do no good to tell. There was no one who would listen nor respond.

Because her sense of Self was denied, Florence had no rudder to navigate the waters of being in intimate relationships. Since she felt powerless and empty, she passively chose relationships with abusive men. Her first marriage was filled with chaos and physical abuse from a raging alcoholic. When he began to hit their child, Florence knew she had to leave, and she moved back home with her father, who reminded her what a loser she was.

Florence's goal then was to find another man and get out of her father's house. She met a man fresh from overseas military deployment. He was not an alcoholic and was very charming. She overlooked the fact that he told dirty jokes and ogled women. She justified his behavior by telling herself that at least he was not an alcoholic.

In this way, she escaped her father's house and had another baby, a daughter. Her new husband also raged and was resentful of her son (now age 7). She, because she couldn't decide what to do, minimized his behavior and stayed in the marriage for 20 years, until she found out he was addicted to online pornography and was seeking other women with whom to chat and exchange pictures. This devastating revelation was perhaps the turning point of her life, which she thought was over.

She put herself in therapy, joined a twelve-step program and found her Self. It took years, another divorce, bodywork, returning to college for her graduate degree, and a new career before Florence was able to feel empowered in herself and deeply connected spiritually. Happily, what was thought to be the end of her life actually became the beginning. Eventually, in addition to finding herself and her spirituality, she found a new and fulfilling relationship.

We each have within us a vital part I call the true Self. As we grow older and the ego comes online, we lose touch with this part of ourselves. To know yourself is to wake up to this part and to recognize when you are thinking and acting from an ego state and when you are thinking and acting from the state of your true Self.

The true Self is the part that is connected to your divine essence. When you are neglected, certain parts of your true Self become walled off, shut down, locked up, closed, tucked away. As a result, certain aspects of your emotional Self remain underdeveloped.

Remember, it is before you were born and during the first and second years of life that your non-verbal, feeling Self developed. If you were neglected during this period of development, it may be more challenging getting to know yourself than it would be in someone who was neglected as an older child, because your neglect happened during a very crucial time of development.

Even if you were not neglected during these crucial early years, any period of childhood development in which you were neglected or abandoned can cause your psyche to develop defense mechanisms to help you avoid pain and not feel.

As an adult, the coping mechanisms (that no longer work!) must be discarded, and sometimes discarding the strategy that helped you survive can be a daunting thing to do. But it is the only way. It is the only way you will be able to say, "This is *my* story. This is *my* hero's journey. This is *my* true Self."

Chapter 14
Addictions

The definition of addiction: "Continued use or behaviors despite adverse consequences"

As a young boy, Johnny spent a lot of time in his room. He read at an early age and amused himself by reading adventure comics on the top bunk of his bed and playing video games. Mother stayed in bed much of the day unless she got up to prepare a meal (which she seldom did) or to "doll up" for Dad when he arrived home from work (which she often did.) Johnny thought his mother was beautiful, and he couldn't figure out what he had done to keep her from getting up and talking to him. He thought he must have been very bad. Often, Johnny was hungry when his mother was asleep, so he climbed as quietly as he could onto the counter to reach the cabinet with peanut butter and grape jelly and bread so he could make himself a sandwich.

Dad worked late and often didn't get home until 7 or 8 o'clock at night. Often, the family would have takeout or fast food for dinner. They ate in front of the TV. These were Johnny's favorite times – just sitting between his mother and father and watching

TV in silence. Twice, Mom went away for a week for a stay at the hospital. When he asked his dad why Mom stayed in bed and went away sometimes, Dad explained that Mom just wasn't feeling well and their family didn't talk about such things. Johnny was instructed to never talk to anyone about Mom's behavior. Dad appeared hurt and angry when Johnny asked about it, and said he was doing the best he could. Johnny never asked again. Even when John was an adult, her illness was not discussed.

When Johnny was 8, he happened upon some pictures of beautiful naked women in the magazines that Dad kept in the garage. He felt strange feelings that he had never felt before. Johnny discovered that by touching his penis he could feel less lonely and he could forget about what a horrible boy he was. He began to spend more and more time in his room masturbating to the sight of the beautiful women in his father's magazines.

By the time the adult John came to therapy, he knew his mother suffered from a severe mental illness and that he (John) had an addiction to masturbating to pornography. He thought his masturbation and pornography use would stop after marrying his college sweetheart, but it did not. Over and over he tried to control the urges, but nothing worked.

When his wife caught him looking at pornography for the third time in a month, she insisted he get help if she was to stay in the marriage. She also sought help for herself to understand why John had lost interest in being physically intimate with her. She was completely devastated that John seemed to prefer looking at pornography over making love to her. She was also furious. John was clear about the fact that he loved his wife and two small children and was terrified about his lack of control over pornography and the possibility of losing his family.

Initially, John began therapy for problems in his marriage. In the first session, John reported he had a happy childhood. He stated that his dad provided well for the family, his mother was caring and kind. There was no abuse of any kind, and everyone did the best they could. However, there were large chunks of his childhood that he could not remember.

Because there were no signs of outward abuse, John failed to see that his psyche had shut down his feelings of deep loneliness and self-blame, and that he'd replaced his emotional pain with pornography and masturbation. When he was acting out with pornography, he could shut out the painful feelings and go into an altered state of consciousness. But afterward, he always felt ashamed that he had once again lied to his wife and broken the promises he had made to himself never to do it again.

Although John was now grown and in his thirties, he sometimes talked and behaved like a much younger person. After college, he got a job with a large corporation but failed to get promoted time after time. He was not especially happy in his job but stated he didn't know what else to do. He felt his father was disappointed in him for not being more aggressive and successful in his work. He reported feeling a sense of dread about going to work.

In conjunction with therapy, John became involved in a twelve-step sexual recovery program where he learned to control his impulses to view pornography one day at a time. Gradually, he established authentic relationships with men like himself who suffered from sexual addiction. He began to allow himself to feel and to name what he was feeling. This was all new to John – this process of letting his emotions come to the surface and honoring them. Before, all he could name that he felt was anger and shame. Beyond anger and shame, he had shut down the emotional side of himself and become numb.

John had developed the strategy of masturbating to pornography in order to stay numb. As with most childhood strategies to stave off feelings and, therefore, pain, he found that there were disastrous consequences in his adult life. He discovered that he was unable to stop the coping mechanism that had worked when he was a child. Now, parts of him were still a child trapped in a man's body.

In therapy, John experienced for the first time someone who sat with him and unconditionally accepted him as he told his painful story. Being heard by a therapist and by his group of twelve-step members was vital for his healing journey.

In a follow-up therapy group John attended after getting sober from pornography, he addressed with other men the trauma of his childhood. In group, he allowed his inner child to speak. From the perspective of his four-year-old Self, he expressed his desperate need to be loved and noticed by his mommy. It was an "aha" experience for John to hear his inner Self speak of his pain. For the first time, he was able to open up and weep for the little boy who blamed himself because his mother could not be there for him.

The don't talk, don't feel rule was broken. And breaking the rule rid the horrid secret of his mother's illness of its awful power. This was not the end of the story for John, of course. He did a great deal of work on his marriage, found a Higher Power that fit his worldview, did more family of origin work, and finally was able to put to rest the idea that he was worthless. He now continues his recovery by passing his experience, strength, and hope to others on their own recovery journey.

This is just one example of the neglect that often occurs when a parent has a serious mental illness. Johnny was told that Dad was doing the best he could and that "our family doesn't talk about such things." Consequently, he was shut down – he had no one he could talk to about questions he had, or feelings he had. The adults in his life were not openly abusive, but they were not really there, either. And his psyche found a way for him to escape – a method that worked adequately in childhood and adolescence but stopped working when he became an adult.

When we begin to wake up and realize the neglect and possible abuse of our childhood, and we determine what strategy or pattern of behavior took hold for us to survive, we may realize that this pattern has escalated into an addictive behavior and is no longer serving us. Therefore, the natural reaction is to be repulsed by it, to want to get rid of it.

Some people, before they even realize it, will go to great lengths to rid themselves of this addiction to a substance or a behavior. Examples of this are:

- Pouring alcohol down the drain
- Flushing drugs down the toilet

- Avoiding drinking/using friends
- Destroying a computer so they can't look at any more porn
- Destroying their ID cards so they can't get into bars, strip clubs, etc.
- Forcing themselves to throw up after overeating
- Quitting a job to avoid the stress or coworkers who participate in or facilitate the addiction
- Moving across the country to get a fresh start

These methods of changing behavior and mood often work for a short while, but usually the behavior either returns or comes out sideways in the form of another addiction or pattern of behavior that is not life-enhancing. Dr. Patrick Carnes calls this phenomenon "Addiction Interaction Disorder." [9]

Addiction Interaction Disorder happens because addictions are coping mechanisms for dealing with emotional (and sometimes physical) pain. We don't want to feel stress, depression, anxiety, loneliness, boredom, and the pain of early-life neglect and trauma, so we learn, over time, to escape these feelings with an addictive behavior or substance. The addiction becomes our primary way of making it through the day without coming apart at the seams. Thus we see that addictions are not about feeling good, they're about feeling less. Addictions are used to escape.

That is why an addict cannot expect to white-knuckle it forever. The "pink cloud" of not using or acting out in your addiction will carry you for a short while, but eventually the painful feelings wrought by early-life neglect, trauma, and other issues will resurface, in full force,

---

9   Carnes, P.J., Murray, R.E., & Charpentier, L. (2004). "Addiction interaction disorder." In R.H. Coombs (Ed.), *Handbook of addictive disorders: A practical guide to diagnosis and treatment* (pp. 31-59). John Wiley & Sons.

and you will find yourself wanting (or needing) to escape. And the easiest way you know to do that is to return to your addiction. These feelings (cravings) are incredibly compelling, even when you know that your addiction no longer serves you and that it may in fact be making your life much worse.

Because of this dynamic, recovering addicts need help and support and a clear understanding of the course of action necessary to begin a new life—a life that fits with their newly formed goals for healing and personal fulfillment. This can involve addiction-focused therapy, 12-step recovery, religious and other addiction-focused support groups, and discovering and nurturing your inner Self.

With regards to your inner Self, what I am going to suggest may sound counterintuitive. However, it makes sense when you understand the reasoning behind it. The first step in discovering and embracing your inner Self is to recognize that we are all human. Being human means that we are not perfect.

Our bodies are part of the whole of who we are. We are mind, spirit, and *body*. In the distant past, religion taught us that our bodies are vile and sinful and to be rejected. However, new ways of believing say that our Creator made us as marvelous creatures with all kinds of ways of adapting and surviving.

Some of those ways work well for us for a time, and then they turn on us. Addictions are a case in point. If you've become addicted, you may be disgusted by some of the things you have done, and you may know very clearly that don't want to do those things anymore. But you must remember that your psyche has no morals about helping you survive your painful childhood. Your psyche's only job when you were a child was to provide an escape from pain that threatened your survival. The ways your psyche found to cope may have worked well too when you were a child. But with an addictive substance or behavior what started as a survival mechanism eventually became your destroyer.

Nevertheless, when you go back and get in touch with your inner Self, you need to be thankful that your psyche, even though it led you to addictive substances and/or behaviors, helped you survive. Then you can explain to yourself that you are now a grown up (or attempting to become a grown up) and you don't need the coping mechanism of your addiction to help you in that way anymore. The addiction is destroying you and interfering with your attempts to live a healthy life, and you are ready to learn healthier ways of making it through the day.

So, give your psyche another job to do. This job will vary depending on the age of your inner child and the circumstances of your childhood, so you will have to do some exploration of what will and won't work for you. As you progress in your Self-knowledge and recovery, you will eventually be able to get into the driver's seat of the bus that your wounded child has commandeered for so many years. You can tell that wounded inner child to go somewhere else and play and be carefree, that you don't need it to be in control anymore because you can take care of yourself.

Please don't take the idea that "you can take care of yourself" as indicating that you can now *control your addiction* without help from others. Many people who have started 12-step recovery or addiction-focused therapy, be it individual or group, make little progress because they refuse to give up the belief that they can, by sheer force of will, control their addiction. In fact, lack of control is the essence of being an addict. To this end, step 1 in 12-step recovery reads: "We admitted we were powerless over our addiction—that our lives had become unmanageable."

Chapter 15
Feelings

Calvin was the youngest of seven brothers in a large, strictly religious family. He grew up in a small town where his family was well-known. When he was 4, his father was killed in a tragic accident. His mother, who was considered a paragon of virtue, handled her depression and grief by increasing her involvement in church. Calvin's brothers handled their anger and grief by beating up on him, usually when he was left alone with them. There was no provision to help the boys access their own feelings or to talk through their own pain. As often happens, these feelings came out sideways in the form of violence, depression, and addiction.

When Calvin told his mother that his brothers hit him, she told them to leave Calvin alone and brushed it off as "all brothers fight and I can't deal with it." Of course, the harassment and hitting continued as soon as her back was turned. Calvin couldn't figure out why, except to tell himself that something was terribly wrong with him that he was so hated. As a teenager, after his grades began to plummet, he was sent away to boarding school, which he did not like.

As an adult, Calvin became a high functioning alcoholic. After getting into recovery, he was left to deal with the pain of feeling no one was there for him. In time, he realized that this was the pain that alcohol allowed him to numb. Through AA, he found kindred spirits who helped him discover his own self-worth, and to see how he was neglected and abused as a child after his father's death. He began to understand that he was not provided proper protection from his abusive brothers and he was scape-goated by being sent away when he became depressed.

Sometimes if neglected children spend time at the homes of their friends' families and those families are attentive and loving, they get a glimpse of what it feels likes to be in a healthier environment than their own. But usually it seems as if they are viewing the other, healthier family through a window and they are not part of it. They know they do not belong to this healthier family, and it hurts to think about wanting a family like that. So they decide to not feel this pain, often by telling themselves that what they've seen in the other family is a sham.

Because of this, neglected and abused children, when they become adults, tend to distrust when things begin to improve in their lives or when someone comes along who can actually see them and be there for them. They tell themselves this cannot last, this is too good to be true, and at any moment things are going to take a turn for the worse and it will all go away.

This is called catastrophic thinking. Having learned that emotions are not safe and are overwhelming, these individuals feel neither sadness nor joy. Life is just one big emotional salad that has been swallowed and pushed down deep inside.

When neglected people begin to feel and name their feelings as part of the healing process, they can feel what it is like to be carefree and joyful, but usually only after going through the pain, sadness, fear, and anxiety of what was buried in the past—neglect, abuse, etc.

If you are someone who has been neglected and only feels numb, I encourage you to allow yourself to get professional help to guide and support you in taking the hero's journey of finding your emotions and discovering that life can be good. Without this help, you may become overwhelmed by the experience of long-buried emotions.

PAYING ATTENTION TO FEELINGS

One of the key factors of discovering who we really are is understanding how we feel. Children who have been neglected have been denied what they need to develop feelings (attention, positive regard, mirroring, nurturing). As adults, they find that they lack the ability to call up and name what they are feeling. It's not that the feelings are not there, it's that they have been repressed in the service of survival from the unbearable truth of not feeling love. Love is the root need of all human beings, and these neglected individuals were often missing that from infancy. And at later ages they may have had their authentic feelings repressed by the ignorant comments of an adult.

Here are some examples of this provided by some of my clients:

1) When a 4-year-old falls down and skins her knee, she is told by a thoughtless father (presumably with the objective of making her laugh) to "Do that again, I didn't see it the first time." Such comments are cruel and far from funny and may indicate an inability to feel on the part of the adult. When a

child is physically hurt, he or she needs comforting and calm reassurance and proper medical care, not callous jokes.

2) A 14-year-old complains to his mother of a severe stomach ache and he is told to stop making such a big deal out of it, it must have been something he ate, and to go lie down. The child actually had a ruptured appendix and was made to feel ashamed for being such a bother. (This example goes beyond the bounds of simple neglect and crosses the line into abusive neglect.)

3) When a child is tired and cranky, she is told to "stop that crying or I'll give you something to cry about." This is a worn-out statement from yesteryear, stemming from the abusive adage that children should be seen and not heard.

4) A child becomes angry at his sister for playing with his favorite toy and breaking it. His mother says that he should be nice and share with his sister and that it is wrong for him to be angry.

5) A child's father uses the statement, "People won't like you if…." What follows are comments like, "If you don't smile, or you're too fat, or you're not nice, or you get angry, or you cry, or you don't clean up after yourself, or you talk about what goes on inside our family, the people won't love you." Statements like these are nothing more than manipulation of the child's feelings and behavior. What child does not want to be liked or loved? And what does the child learn? The child learns to be nicey-nice, compliant, and to repress who he or she really is and what he or she is really feeling. A variation on this same theme is, "What will people think?"

6) When a 6-year-old child's mother dies, his aunt tells him that he has to be a brave boy and wash his face, go to his room, and play quietly.

7) When a 12-year-old boy's father runs off with another woman, his distraught and dependent mother tells him that

he will have to be the man of the house now. Six months later, when his father returns home, the boy is left with his rage and confusion about being kicked back to the role of a child. Since it is not permissible to show anger, the boy's feelings are repressed, and they reside like a brick within him.

Feelings are our body's way of releasing pent-up emotion. Children who are not able to express their emotions soon learn to not pay attention to their feelings, and then they lose touch with their inner Self. Overcoming this can be a difficult process.

When a client in the process of healing is able to first show emotion, that person will sometimes apologize to me, especially if he or she starts to cry. I respond by telling the client that there is nothing to apologize for, and then I congratulate the client for finally letting his or her long pent-up emotions out.

When you're healing from neglect, expressing emotions may seem overwhelming in the beginning since those emotions have been deeply repressed for such a long time. However, when these emotions finally start to surface, the process of the seemingly eternal work of mourning the loss of what was needed, but never received, has begun.

Chapter 16
Extending Self-Care to Food

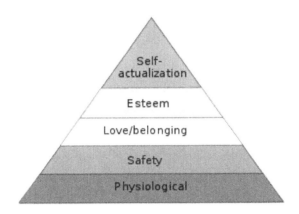

Maslow's Hierarchy of Needs is a pyramid that reminds us to begin with a foundation of taking care of our physical bodies before moving up the pyramid through the concepts of safety, love/belonging, esteem, and Self-actualization. Our physical needs come first. And without doubt one of those needs is food.

THE POTENTIAL MEANINGS OF FOOD

For many people, food means much more than just physiological survival. Eating—especially sugary, fatty, and/or salty foods—can become a strategy for neglected or overcontrolled children to comfort themselves. They might also come to believe that what they put into their mouths is the *only* form of control they have.

Unfortunately, food taken in for the wrong reasons can lead to either obesity or the opposite, anorexia/bulimia. Add to that the sick, shaming messages that our culture and the advertising industry give us about our acceptability being connected with body size, and we have a big problem.

Originally, food consisted of natural roots, vegetables, legumes, fruits, dairy, and meat. It was meant to nurture and sustain the human body, to provide energy, and to maintain health. Today, food has taken on a whole new meaning. It is often heavily refined and processed, sometimes beyond the point of providing any nutrients at all, which defeats the primary purpose of eating it. But we still eat it, because for some of us, especially if we've been neglected, food has become a way to fill the emptiness within.

Here are some scenarios where neglect has created an unhealthy understanding of and relationship with food:

- Food is used as a reward, especially junk food and candy. "If you're good, I'll give you a candy bar."
- Food is used to punish or control. Examples include: "You were bad, so you don't get any dessert." "You will sit at the table and eat your liver and onions, young lady. I don't care if you have to sit there all night. So quit your crying." "Clean your plate; think of the starving children in Africa. You should be ashamed." "We're so happy that the new baby is now trained to wait four hours between feedings. We just let him cry until it is feeding time." "Don't eat anything between meals, you'll ruin your dinner!"

- Food is used to shame. "That will make you fat. People won't like you if you're fat." "You look like you're gaining weight." "You ought to be ashamed of yourself for not eating everything your mother serves you." "What do you mean you don't like that? There must be something wrong with you."

You get the picture. Food takes on a whole new meaning when it is paired with neglectful and hurtful statements and behaviors that induce fear and shame. Power can be exerted over a child by all the rhetoric about being obese and/or anorexic, or uncaring about others who might be starving, or weird for not liking a certain type of food. In the end, of course, it all becomes tied to not being properly loved and cared for.

There are thousands of methods of weight loss, including supplements, prescription drugs, over the counter medications, diets, exercise regimens, and more. Often, these methods and even registered dietitians do not take into account the problem of our emotional connection to food. The advice to "just eat fruits and vegetables and avoid sweets and fatty foods" does not fix the problem because it does not address the *real* problem of unresolved neglect and abuse. The way food is used for purposes other than nutrition has to be examined.

The acronym HALT is often used to help people determine why they are eating. HALT is an acronym that stands for, "Are you 1) Hungry? 2) Angry? 3) Lonely? Or 4) Tired?" Remembering to HALT before eating helps us to eat mindfully. It forces us to ask ourselves, "Am I really hungry, or am I trying to stuff my feelings?" If we are hungry, we should eat. If we are not hungry, we can nurture ourselves in other ways. And as we eat we can ask, "Am I full now or do I want another bite?" If the answer is yes, then we should take another bit. If the answer is no, we should stop.

Usually, just eating slowly helps us to be in touch with our bodies and to know when we are full. In our rushed and pressured society, however, we are encouraged to wolf down our food, which causes us to be completely out of touch with when we are full. Rushed eating is mindless eating. Slowing down and staying aware while we are eating is an important part of recognizing our immediate needs and knowing our inner selves.

Chapter 17
Moving Your Body

Another physiological aspect of Self-care involves physical movement and exercise (expending the calories that we take in). We need to burn off the food we eat, or we gain unhealthy weight and become sluggish both physically and mentally.

It may not appeal to you to spend hours working out at a gym. If so, that's OK. You don't have to go to the gym to exercise. The idea is to move your body. Stretching, walking, bicycling, dancing, Tai Chi, Qi Gong, and countless other activities are all valid forms of moving your body.

You may find that you want to work out alone or that you prefer to exercise with a group. If you do not already have an exercise regimen that you enjoy, I suggest that you investigate what is available in your area. Usually, there are groups that go for a walk every morning, or a hike every weekend. And there are swim classes, yoga classes, sports leagues, and hundreds of other activities that help you to enjoy the movement that keeps you healthy.

If you're out of shape, start small and work up to 3 or 4 days a week with at least 30 minutes of exercise. This is especially important if you have a job that is sedentary. When you do this, you will be surprised at how much better you feel. Not only do your aches and pains diminish, you become sharper mentally and happier because exercise wakes up your brain and produces depression-reducing endorphins.

Part Four
Steps to Regaining Consciousness

"And the day came when the risk to remain tight in a bud was more painful than the risk it took to blossom."

Anais Nin

Chapter 18
A Daily Practice

One of the most effective ways of going inside yourself and getting to know who you are is to spend daily time in some sort of mindfulness meditation. Whether you do this first thing in the morning or last thing before bedtime (or both), you should find a special place where you will not be disturbed. You may have to inform other members of the household that this is your "quiet time" and to please not interrupt you for a certain period of time.

CREATING YOUR QUIET SPACE

It is usually helpful to go to the same spot each time you meditate. If you are fortunate enough to have a special room where you can be alone, then you can decorate it in a way that creates a mood of serenity and calm. You can add items that enhance your meditation experience such as candles, a diffuser for incense or essential oils like lavender and geranium, and a mala (beads). You can also create a small altar or space on a side table for your journal, a book of inspirational readings, and a small item or picture that holds a special meaning for you. Even if you don't have a space you can dedicate entirely to meditation, a quiet space can be created in the corner of your bedroom or guest room. Just be sure there is a comfortable place to sit and a positive, peaceful feel to it.

WHAT DO I DO?

If you are new to meditation, it may feel challenging at first. I encourage you to experiment with different types of meditation to find what feels right for you. There are many good books on meditating and even apps, such as "Calm" and "Headspace," that can help you with this.

When you are just starting out, forget about any special postures, just be comfortable. Be gentle, pay attention to your breath, treasure silence. Start with just 10 minutes, which will feel like an eternity when you start. Don't *expect* anything. Just be. And accept that you will have many thoughts while you meditate. That's normal. Welcome them and let them float by like clouds. Ending with an inspirational reading is helpful—some positive and uplifting thought you can take with you back into your daily routine. Most importantly, breathe!

Your goal with a daily practice of meditation is to set the intention to go within yourself, and to do it every day. As you practice, you may want to increase your time and to journal your thoughts and feelings.

Discovering the method by which you survived and the associated feelings is a primary goal in becoming aware of why you do the things you do. This is vitally important in Self-discovery. It is only when you know what certain feelings are *really* about and why certain behaviors developed, that you can begin to take charge of your life. It is likely that you will find, if you are dedicated to some form of daily meditation, that this effort helps you greatly in this regard.

You came into this world with the natural mechanism of crying that let your mother or father know you needed something (including their presence and loving touch.) And you may have cried and screamed and yelled, but nothing happened. As you got older, you may have learned to make them laugh or do something "cute" or something clever to get their attention. You may have taken care of them as if they were the child. You may have excelled in sports or dance or some activity that brought attention. You may have been very obedient and remained very quiet and become very small so as not to upset them. You may have given up and stayed away from home, running the neighborhood in search of friends or the family of friends who would pay attention to you. You may have become the scapegoat, getting negative attention from teachers, authority figures, and parents who labeled you the problem child. You may have developed a rich interior life of fantasy and made up magical stories of how your life was or was going to be. You may have turned to alcohol or drugs or porn or some other addictive behavior.

Through it all, you shut down your inner needs and learned not to trust anyone. Or you became numb to your sense of discernment about who was safe, and you trusted everyone who would pay attention to you. However you learned to survive, you were silently screaming "Please see me."

A daily practice of meditation can help you see this, to feel this, and to let your anger and shame about this pass through your mind and heart and out of your body. And when that anger and shame is cleared away, continued meditation can help you find your true Self.

SIT WITH YOUR FEELINGS

Most people who have been neglected have learned to avoid feelings. Now that you know you were neglected and are working on it, you may find that in your quiet time you suddenly feel your emotions, some of which are likely to be painful. Your natural desire will be to push them away. Instead, as you meditate, you can allow yourself to gently notice them—perhaps as if you are outside yourself. When you do this, just sit with them. Let them be. You might even welcome them, understanding that they are being given you to make you whole. Be curious about them. Examine the thoughts that come with them. Do they bring to your remembrance any incident from your childhood? Are they connected to ways you get triggered in your present life?

Be patient. You are getting to know yourself. Record in your journal what you notice.

JOURNAL

I recommend going to the office supply section of a local store and purchasing a cheap wire-bound lined notebook. It doesn't have to be anything fancy. Record your experiences with your daily meditation practice in this journal.

Your journal can also be used to express anger and frustration. You can curse and just get it out.

Journaling is also for gratitude, new insights, intentions, and affirming yourself. You can write poetry, write prayers, and set goals.

Your journal is your partner in healing. It is *not* for negative hate-filled rhetoric about yourself. That type of writing only will increase your anxiety and delay your healing. So, while your journal is OK for venting, its primary purpose is to help you discover your Self, and to let insights unfold as to why you think and feel and react the way you do.

Lastly, your journal is private and no one else's business. Keep it in a safe place and, unless you are choosing to share it, do not leave it out. This is not "keeping secrets," it's having privacy, which everyone deserves.

AWARENESS OF YOUR PERSONAL SURVIVAL STRATEGY

It is important that you realize that spending time in quiet meditation is the gateway through which you enter the universe that is inside you. If you picture your conscious mind as being like the tip of an iceberg and your unconscious mind—the inner part of your Self—to be the hidden part of the iceberg that is under the water, this will give you a visual image of just how vast and mysterious that as yet unknown part of your Self is.

It is in meditation that you enter your unconscious mind and discover the ways in which you learned to survive and why you developed these coping mechanisms (that no longer serve you). You will come to understand that even before you could speak, you absorbed your parents' energy, and you learned to read their faces, interpret their tone of voice, their gestures. That is, when they were physically present. You will come to understand that you tried different methods to get the attention you so desperately needed. When one didn't work, you tried another. When one did work, you internalized it and used it again and again to get the crumbs of attention that helped you go on. It is in meditation that you discover what you unconsciously learned about your mother and father that helped you get by.

As you notice your Self in meditation, pay attention to where it hurts in your body. How did you learn to survive/avoid the pain? Record this in your journal.

Chapter 19
Stay In the Now

Eckhart Tolle is probably the best-known person to write about "the power of now." This concept of living one day at a time has been around in 12-step recovery for a long time. Major religions also embrace this concept. Buddhism teaches present moment mindfulness. Jesus taught us to "take no thought for tomorrow because tomorrow will have worries of its own." Lao Tsu tells us that "the journey of a thousand miles begins with a single step." All of these teachings point to the same concept—that living in the present moment is the way to become and stay whole.

This does not mean we should ignore the past. The past is great for teaching us what not to do again, to help us learn what worked and what didn't work, and to help us recognize our shortcomings and perhaps to make amends for them so we can effectively move on.

People who have suffered trauma in the past may have the symptoms of Post-Traumatic Stress Disorder (PTSD), meaning they obsess about and are triggered by past traumas over and over in response to events occurring in the present. If you find yourself stuck in the past over some traumatic event and you cannot bring yourself back to the present, it would be wise to seek professional help to determine what is going on and to heal it. Otherwise, the past will continue to rule your present.

And yes, neglect is a form of trauma that needs to be healed in this way.

The future presents similar challenges because neglected and abused people tend to attach the present situation to past events and assume/fear that the negative situation will repeat itself in the future. This is a form of anxiety. Sometimes people in 12-step groups will refer to this as "living in the wreckage of the future."

When children are neglected, they learn not to expect too much, and that they have to do things for themselves because no one is going to be there for them. Often, because they are still children and their brains are not fully developed, they make poor choices that lead to negative outcomes. As adults, they may teach themselves to deny or minimize traumatic childhoods by telling themselves that it wasn't so bad after all, while living in a constant state of anxiety—waiting for (and expecting) things to go awry. When life does bring happy and joyful events, they engage in catastrophic thinking because this is how they learned to think. They have come to believe that if they expect the worst, they will avoid disappointment.

In your daily meditation practice and throughout the day, pay attention to whether you are thinking about some past event or projecting into the future. If you are doing one or both of these, you can consciously choose to bring your focus back to the present moment and to think about what is right in front of you. Sometimes people ask themselves, "Where are my feet," and this helps them to stay in or return to the now.

As you work on staying in the moment, be patient with yourself, as this focus will need to be done over and over. Your old habit of focusing on the past and the future, rather than the now, is deeply ingrained and will not be easily broken.

Chapter 20
Simplify Your Life

Many people who have been neglected avoid the concept of having a daily mindfulness practice, or they claim they tried it and "it didn't work." One of the most universal reasons people don't try or discontinue daily meditation is that they "don't have the time." In this respect, our culture is not geared toward individuals becoming Self-aware.

Yes, our lives are very busy, especially if there are still children at home. And society encourages us to fill every moment with some activity, amusement, or task that is deemed *important*. When our days are filled with an overly long to-do list, there is little or no time left for introspection. Yet this vital healing tool is so much more important than watching the final episode of some mindless (or even intelligent) TV show.

I know that right now you are probably saying, "You don't understand. First, I don't sleep that well to begin with. Then I get up before dawn to work out, grab something to eat, shower, shave, get the kids up and off to school, and drive to work. And after work I race home and help with dinner and clean-up and the kids' homework, and after all of that I *need* to relax and zone out with something mindless like TV." Or maybe you're saying, "I didn't sleep well last night because one of the kids was sick. Then I got up early to prepare lunches, fix breakfast, get the kids up and ready for school. After that I had to get my hair cut, and then after school, I went to my son's soccer game, picked my daughter up from school play rehearsal, fed them, and helped them both with their homework. Then we had baths and bedtime. So when exactly am I supposed to slow down and meditate?"

By the time we get through the "must do" tasks of our day, most of us are exhausted and just want to fall into bed. If we don't have kids, we have pets and a variety of other people who need our time. Things like Self-care and even emotional and sexual intimacy can easily take a back seat to all the other activities that are begging for our attention. Sometimes, if we're part of a couple, we have to add "date night" into our schedules as a kind of appointment.

We must not forget to add in the relatives. Sometimes our parents— the very people who once neglected us—are now retired and needy and suddenly want to be involved in our lives, often by offering unsolicited advice and asking for time-eating favors.

If we are involved in a religious community, there are the church services to attend, and the church which needs volunteers to teach Sunday School, clean the sanctuary, sponsor the Youth Group, lead Bible Studies, and help with all sorts of other tasks.

Still, we find time for TV, movies, video games, social media, and stuffing our faces with junk food or cocktails as a way to numb out at the end of a busy day.

I have listed just a few of the ways in which our days can get filled to the point of ignoring our own need for aloneness and meditation. Of course, none of the things listed above are bad in and of themselves. Children and pets do require time and attention. And it is a good thing to be involved in a healthy way with parents and siblings and spirituality. These are all foundational aspects of a well-rounded life. But when does enough become more than enough?

If you don't have time to spend with your inner Self and your life completely revolves around everything that is happening "out there," you are out of balance and will remain asleep to your true Self. In such cases, you must find ways to say no to activities that do not enhance your intention of healing from neglect. This is an essential task of healing. Otherwise, as John Bradshaw said, we become human doings, not human beings.

To begin to pare down your activities, I suggest you take the time to make a list of the things you do and divide it into three columns. Column One lists the things that absolutely, unequivocally have to be done; Column Two lists the things that enhance your life but are not essential; Column Three reveals things that do not enhance your life and that may actually keep you stuck in meaningless routines.

Sit with this list and carefully consider which things do and do not line up with your inner guidance system, even though you may not fully know your inner guidance system at this time. Notice how you *feel* about each item. If you find yourself feeling shame, pressure, anxiety, or anger about anything on the list, think about how you can change that feeling. If the activity cannot be dropped, how can you accept it? For example, you may have to accept that you cannot change a situation or another person, but you *can* change yourself and what you are willing to do.

After you have eliminated some of the non-essential things on your daily to-do list, notice that you now have more time for yourself. The tendency will be to procrastinate in setting aside time for Self-care, or, conversely, to fill your extra time with some other non-essential activity. If you find yourself falling into this trap, it's important to remember that you have done the work of making this list so you can have the time to take care of yourself. And you are doing this because you have committed to getting to know the wonderful person that you are—the valuable human being who is worth knowing.

SPACE

What does your desk look like? What does your closet look like? What does your car look like? How do you feel and what do you say to yourself when you see your desk, your closet, your car? Many people don't give clutter a second thought. Others obsess about it and constantly keep things neat. Still others say negative things to themselves when they pass by the clutter, yet feel too overwhelmed to do anything about it.

Whichever kind of person you are, it is a fact that our culture is obsessed with having more and bigger things. Because of this, you can amass so much stuff that your stuff runs your life, rather than your being able to calmly enjoy the stuff that you have.

Some people think if they only had (fill in the blank), they would be happy. Then they find this is not the case at all. Things, whatever they are, need attention, time, and maintenance if they are to be used and enjoyed. Fancy cars and fancy homes and expensive toys must be kept up or they lose their appeal and value. And plenty of other things are no longer useful to us at all. Examples of this are clothes that no longer fit or are out of style, things that don't bring us joy,, gadgets that are never used, and decorations that don't fit your home anymore. All of these things take up space in our mind and our living environment, adding to our anxiety.

Keeping our lives de-cluttered and thoughtfully considering a purchase before making that purchase helps keep us free from the control that our things have over us. These practices also provide us with space, both in our minds and our environment. Space that helps us breathe more freely.

I encourage you to regularly rid yourself of the things you have that do not contribute to your wellbeing. Usually, it is best to do this gently, one item at a time. Don't be afraid of throwing something away, giving it away, or recycling it. Be aware of the *meaning* a material object has for you and think about why you are keeping it. Then decide for yourself what to do, always keeping in mind that you are the one in charge here.

Chapter 21
Connect

THE BUTTERFLY EFFECT

This term, coined by Edward Lorenz, is derived from the metaphorical example of the details of a tornado (the exact time of formation, the exact path taken) being influenced by minor perturbations such as the flapping of the wings of a distant butterfly several weeks earlier. Over time, this phenomenon has been generalized to mean that even one small action produces universal results. As such, all living things are connected and our behaviors, and even our thoughts, can have monumental consequences.

It is an accepted fact that humans are wired for connection. Patients experiencing depression, anxiety, severe trauma, and grief are encouraged to be around safe, supportive people. But what if the ones with whom we are surrounded are shut down, critical, negative, and not available to us emotionally? Then the loneliness becomes even more painful.

Our society prides itself on social media, networking, collaboration, get-togethers, hanging out, group meetings, team sports, and community events. One would think humans would be more than fulfilled with connections and only need a little space alone once in a while to achieve a sense of balance. Unfortunately, this is not always the case. And when it is not the case, the butterfly effect may be in play, with a small amount of disconnection in one area turning into a large amount of disconnection elsewhere.

SOCIAL MEDIA

Social media sites like Facebook, Instagram, Snapchat, Me-We, Twitter, and the like are hugely popular digital venues designed to catch and hold one's attention by stimulating the feel-good chemicals in our brains. If you're on one of these sites, you already know that it feels good when someone "likes" or "loves" your post or comment. It's great that you can post pictures of your latest meal at a fancy restaurant and have all your friends comment "yummmmm" and that they always seem to "like" the cute pics of your kitties. It's also great that you can do the same for them.

Even more stimulating for some people –are political posts. If you agree with a post, then you feel good; if not, you can feel righteous anger at the stupidity of the post, and then you can make a snide comment about it.

Jaron Lanier, a computer philosophy writer, scientist and founding father of virtual reality, gave a TEDx talk in which he stresses that Facebook and Google are designed to addict users.[10] I am assuming every other social media platform and online game is set up in a similar way. Not to mention the online pornography industry. This addiction occurs because of the "hits" of feel-good chemicals they are designed to induce.

---

10   Lanier, J. (2018). Jaron Lanier: How we need to remake the internet [Video file]. Retrieved from https://www.ted.com/talks/jaron_lanier_how_we_need_to_remake_the_internet.

Nevertheless, social media allows you to connect with long lost school friends, participate in a GoFundMe page, give and receive helpful advice, etc. So social media is a good thing to a point. However, it is not such a good thing when viewed as a platform to gain close friends.

We call people Facebook friends (or Twitter friends, or whatever), but are they really friends? A real friend, is someone whom Dr. Brené Brown calls a "Move Your Body" friend. "Move Your Body" friends show up to move through the depths with you. They say, "All right! Let's do this thing. I'm with you, I've done it. Let's talk it through." This is someone who has earned the right to hear your shame and to tell you the truth about what they hear.[11] A real friend will not judge you, will not pass your information on as juicy gossip, will not flatter you by telling you what you would like to hear instead of the truth. A real friend will not give unsolicited advice for which you did not ask. A real friend will be there for you when things fall apart and rejoice with you when things are good. A real friend will not be offended if much time goes by between times you communicate, and both of you can pick up right where you left off when you do connect. A real friend will not put up with your crap, will appropriately tell you when you are out of line, and will not desert you because of it. If you have one or even two friends like this, you are lucky. They are precious. Hold on to them.

Sometimes people who are already your real friends become your online friends, too. But only rarely do people who start out as online friends become your real friends. That said, social media can still be a place to find meaningful connection, especially for younger people who tend to view digital interactivity as being on par with real-world activity.

---

11   Brown, B. (2010). *The gifts of imperfection: Let go of who you think you're supposed to be and embrace who you are.* Hazelden Publishing.

CHURCH

Churches and other spiritual venues can also be a good place to connect and find support, although for some people these communities are not the best places to find trustworthy friends. Some people feel they have to keep problems to themselves because, after all, they are people of faith and their lives are saved now. So they put on a happy face and pretend all is well, avoiding crying in church except in reaction to an inspirational hymn that brings tears of joy.

And even church people can betray your trust. I am reminded of a sweet woman who inadvertently contracted a deadly STD from an unfaithful boyfriend. She confided to her best friend at church, who promised to protect the information but instead shared it with other church members. Shockingly, this dear woman was labeled a "sinner" and shunned. She was so heartbroken that she eventually chose to leave the church.

For the most part, however, spiritual communities are supportive and nurturing, and good places to connect.

TWELVE-STEP RECOVERY

Marjorie came to therapy for problems in her marriage to Stan, who was an active alcoholic. This was her second marriage, the first being to another alcoholic who physically abused her. She denied experiencing any childhood trauma or abuse.

Marjorie grew up in a large city with one brother who was twelve years older than herself. Her parents owned a bar and an ice house, which were located next to the family home. Marjorie felt as if she were really an only child, as her brother joined the Air Force by the time she was 5 and rarely came home. Dad was an active alcoholic who was jovial and fun when he was drunk. He often made sarcastic jokes putting down other people. Mom was the responsible one in the marriage, running the bar and taking care of practically every aspect of the family's life.

In therapy, Marjorie described her mom as kind and caring. Dad was like a child and Mom took care of him. Dad could not really be there for Marjorie, because he was impaired by the alcohol. Mom tried to be there for Marjorie but running the business and house, plus caring for Dad sapped Mom of any energy she would have left for Marjorie.

Marjorie's parents worked at the bar from as early as she could remember, but she was told that Mom had stayed home with her until she was 4. Mom came home once or twice every evening to make sure Marjorie was OK, to sit her in front of the TV for company, and to get her ready for bed. After 2 a.m., when the bar closed, Mom and Dad would come home. Marjorie put herself to bed every night.

The TV became Marjorie's babysitter. In school, Marjorie made good grades, but at home no one noticed. Mom was focused on Dad's drinking and keeping him in line. When Marjorie was 12, she saw an evangelist on TV who encouraged her to give her life to Jesus, which she did right there in the living room when her parents were gone. The next day she asked if she could go down the street to the Baptist church.

Marjorie was happy to attend church by herself but felt confused when the preacher talked about sin and the evils of drinking alcohol. She told her mother and dad when she got home that Dad shouldn't drink because the preacher said it was wrong. Although her comment was not discussed, Marjorie was not allowed to attend church again. She felt confused and lonely about not being able to attend Sunday School anymore, as it provided the only opportunity she had at the time to explore a world outside her family of origin and the possibility of having a spiritual life. She began to feel depressed, even though she didn't recognize this at the time.

In high school, Marjorie dated many boys but always seemed to be attracted to "the bad boys." She had sex for the first time at a party when she was 15 with a 17-year-old boy. Instantly, she felt she was in love and wanted to marry him. He broke her heart. She continued to date and was sexually active almost immediately with the boys she dated. She felt "real" and loved when she was in a relationship and thought that when a boy had sex with her, that meant he loved her as she loved him.

Marjorie married an abusive alcoholic, something she swore she would never do, when she was 18. After living with his physical abuse for 5 years, she left, only to marry her current husband, Stan, another alcoholic. Stan initially denied having a problem with alcohol, and Marjorie tried to believe him, consoling herself with the fact that he was the life of the party when he was drunk and not physically abusive.

In therapy, Marjorie got in touch with the agonizing loneliness she had felt throughout her life. In addition to Al-anon, she began attending the 12-step program for Adult Children of Alcoholics and found others with whom she could identify. She also realized how unconsciously she was attracted to men like her father, even though she really wanted a deep and intimate relationship.

Marjorie found caring and support in therapy and at 12 step programs. She started taking care of herself in addition to learning healthy ways of interacting with Stan. Stan began attending AA on his own and eventually embraced his recovery. It took much work and time, but Stan and Marjorie began to develop the kind of relationship that both of them really deserved and wanted.

This is a success story, but not all stories turn out this way. Stan decided on his own to change and seek help with the alcoholism he found impossible to fight on his own. Marjorie found the courage to reach out for support and help in her own struggle with living with a spouse who is addicted. Sometimes, when one partner gets healthy and accepts that he or she cannot change the other no matter what, and the other partner doesn't want to change, eventually the healthier partner has to leave the relationship in order to be true to his or her Self.

I have found that one of the best places for neglected individuals to find real friends is at 12-step meetings, regardless of the type. These meetings are made up of hurting people who are drawn there because they are ready to make significant life changes. Still, since people are human, some folks would not be good friends. But many more would be. Usually, these people have walked the road of recovery and have come out changed for the better. Many, if not most, have suffered some form of abuse and neglect. If they are working their own recovery, they will understand your pain and will keep your information confidential.

Therefore, I propose you try a 12-step meeting. Which one? If, while in the process of your daily practice and journaling, you have discovered that you may be addicted to a substance or behavior, then consider the 12-step program that fits the substance or behavior. If you can't identify any substance or behavioral addiction, I would recommend Al-Anon or Adult Children of Alcoholics (ACoA). The reason these are good programs is you do not have to be with an alcoholic or have alcoholic parents to benefit from the support these programs offer. Both of these programs allow you to examine your own life and get into your feelings while getting caring and wise support.

If your parent(s) were addicted to something, consider that someone who is actively drinking or drugging is not capable of being present and real to children. Therefore, neglect. Your parents may have had other reasons that they were not capable of being there for you, but the common denominator in groups like Al-Anon and ACoA is that you were all neglected. Some people in these programs were also abused in unspeakable ways by their childhood caregivers, but foundationally there was neglect.

Don't tell yourself that because your life was "not as bad as others" that you would be making too big of a deal of your problems by attending meetings like this. In fact, this is what almost every person says when he or she starts recovery, regardless of the substance, behavior, or consequences. If you haven't become addicted to some behavior or substance, then you are very fortunate indeed. My guess is when you carefully think about it, you have still learned to cope and survive in one or more ways that don't serve you well now. So my suggestion is that you try 12-step meetings. And not just one meeting, either. Go to at least six.

In all 12-step groups, there is something that is usually said at the end of a meeting. It is, "Keep coming back. It works if you work it, and you're worth it." This may sound like a silly little saying, but I have heard so many active addicts say, "I tried that meeting and it just didn't work for me." Notice that the meeting itself is being blamed for the process not working. Here's the key: Recovery is not a spectator sport. YOU HAVE TO WORK IT. It is not easy, and the hardest part is starting, talking for the first time, and then sticking with it.

Another thing. The frightened part of you will give you every excuse under the sun for not going and/or not sticking with it. However, when you actually start working with a good sponsor (a mentor who helps you work the 12 steps) and experiencing what it is like to work each step, you will be surprised at how your life begins to change. At some point, you will have a moment of awakening, and you will know that you have done the right thing.

If you feel that 12-step recovery is either not for you or you just can't make the commitment to attend a meeting, then please at least consider some sort of therapeutic group experience. During the time you are first discovering your true Self, and while you are discovering and ridding yourself of addictive practices and possibly substances that kept you unconscious of reality, you will need the assistance of others. And there are parts of ourselves and our behaviors that we cannot see but others can. We need positive yet true feedback from others to fully heal. Whether this takes the form of group therapy, an accountability group, a 12-step meeting, or something else, being identified with and part of a group helps us to expand our sense of Self and to see that we are not alone.

A word of caution here. You may not like the first group you try. That's OK. I encourage you to try other groups until you find one that fits your needs. You may not (and probably will not) like everyone in the group you choose, and that too is OK. The point is to find a place where you can openly talk about your stuff.

That said, there are possible pitfalls to being in a group. One is the tendency to think the group is all there is. In other words, it is not wise to adopt all the ideas of the group without discernment. Groups where everyone is the same ethnicity, nationality, or religion run the risk of narrow-minded thinking that is not well balanced. Remember, you are seeking to be mindful and to think for yourself. You don't want the group to become another way for you to avoid finding your true Self.

You need other people. You are made for connection. You are made to know yourself. You are made to be loved and to pass that love on to other people in the form of respect, kindness, generosity, compassion, and acceptance. And you are made to demonstrate these love traits to yourself as well.

Chapter 22
Living in Balance

One of the Universal Laws is called the Law of Opposites. The Earth demonstrates this with the poles, the seasons, gravity (up/down), etc. We all learned this concept in elementary school.

The Law of Opposites is also demonstrated in the behaviors and thoughts that play out when we first begin to change the way we think and act. When we initially begin to awaken to the idea that there is something inside ourselves that we didn't know was there, there is the tendency to act out in the other extreme. If we never allowed ourselves to get angry, we might now get furious and express that inappropriately. If we never allowed ourselves to feel sad or happy or lonely or afraid, we may become overwhelmed with our feelings. (One tough-guy recovering addict laughingly remembers that when he was new to recovery, he cried incessantly, often set off by something as simple as a Hallmark commercial. For him, every emotion was overwhelming to the point where he cried.)

When we experience the Law of Opposites in this way, moving from one extreme to another, the "healing" extreme may be too much for us, causing us to shut ourselves down again. Part of the healing process is learning to ride this roller-coaster while we're on it, and, over time, finding a happy medium. But in the early stages of healing, that happy medium usually is not possible for us.

Similarly, if we are addicted to a behavior, we may go to the other extreme in recovery. Two common behavioral addictions involve sex and food. Because the addictive behavior may have been so shaming and destructive before recovery, our tendency may be to go in the other direction, eliminating sexual activity entirely or borderline starving ourselves by not eating.

With sexual addiction, the protocol is to ask the addict to abstain from sexual activity both with Self and others for a reasonable period of time (usually 30 days to 6 months), but *not* forever. In recovery, the addicted person learns how to have healthy sex because that is a part of being human. Before, the object of the behavior was not to have sex but to shut down uncomfortable feelings. In recovery, the addict learns to be present for himself/herself and his/her partner in an emotional way while not feeling ashamed of sexual desires. For sex addicts, this is a whole new way of being.

With food, addicts must change their entire relationship with eating. Similar to sex, food was not used to satisfy natural hunger, it was compulsively used to shut down feelings, resulting in either obesity or anorexia. As with sexual addiction, "sobriety" with an eating disorder is not about abstinence, it's about learning to engage in the behavior in healthy rather than obsessive, escapist ways.

When we first are courageous enough to actually feel our feelings and to recognize that our childhoods were not so good after all, it is necessary to grieve what we did not have. And we, like the tough guy described above, may fear that the crying will never stop. But it will. Or, because we are not used to crying, we may apologize for having tears in front of others and try to shut them down. But really we are to be congratulated for finally feeling our feelings. Eventually, we may be able to stop the flow of tears, but not now. And we should not try.

Instead, we should remember that there has been a buildup of years of repressed feelings. We are not weak or lacking in any way because we are crying. In fact, this is the way our Creator meant for us to release pent-up emotions. Our feelings and our emotions and our ability to express our feelings and emotions are a gift.

The idea here is to develop balance—to live in the middle way. The middle way is when we are mindful of what is going on inside of us, and we make choices about what we're going to do about it that line up with our inner guidance system. When we do this, we are getting in the driver's seat of our life, and that is a wonderful thing.

Chapter 23
Get Professional Help

MEDICATION

I'm not a big promoter of medication, as it seems Big Pharma is always at the ready with a pill for everything, along with a variety of side effects. However, when one has been traumatized through lack of attachment (neglect), it may be necessary to get on proper medication and maintain it at least for a while. I would suggest getting a full evaluation from a reputable psychiatrist and continuing to be monitored by the psychiatrist.

If you are paying attention to your body, your body will tell you when it is time to seek the help of a psychiatrist. Some prime indicators are insomnia that cannot be corrected with good sleep hygiene and an over-the-counter medication, the urge to isolate because of a lingering feeling of depression, an ever-present feeling of anxiety or fear, extreme changes in mood—going from feeling really great to crashing in crippling depression—spending money you don't have when feeling sad, and making poor judgments by having indiscriminate sex. And, of course, do not hesitate to get help if you are having any thoughts about hurting yourself or someone else. Don't wait until you are actively suicidal before getting an appointment because you may not be able to schedule an office visit right away. Otherwise, you may have to go to the emergency room.

There are a number of effective psychotropic medications available today. You will need to be under the care of a psychiatrist, a medical doctor who specializes in mental health, because each medication affects each individual differently and all medications may have side effects. Do not hesitate to call your psychiatrist if you are having negative side effects from your medication.

PROFESSIONAL THERAPY

Talk Therapy

Examples of basic modalities of talk therapy include CBT (Cognitive Behavioral Therapy), Person-Centered (Rogerian Therapy), Motivational Interviewing, DBT (Dialectical Behavioral Therapy), and Short-Term Brief Psychotherapy. There are so many methods of doing talk therapy now that it may seem confusing to the layperson who has not previously been in therapy.

The important thing for you, as a neglected person, to remember is that talk therapy provides you with a caring professional who is an active listener. Most people who were neglected as children never had anyone that they could trust and with whom they could share their pain and their story. Therapy is the opposite of this. Whichever modality is used, your therapist can assist you by hearing your pain and helping you find your way out of the pain.

Dialectical Behavior Therapy (DBT)

Dialectical Behavior Therapy (DBT) is a cognitive behavioral treatment developed by Marsha Linehan, PhD, ABPP. It emphasizes individual psychotherapy and group skills training. The goal is to help people learn and use new skills and strategies to develop a life that they experience as worth living. DBT skills include skills for mindfulness, emotion regulation, distress tolerance, and interpersonal effectiveness. It is a specific treatment for individuals who suffer from the inability to regulate their emotions.

Radically Open Dialectical Behavior Therapy (DBT)

Most clinical treatments have been developed for clients who struggle with a lack of self–control in various areas of their lives. These under-controlled clients often benefit from evidence-based treatments that provide structure and emotional regulation. However, some clients are struggling with over-control. These more clients do not respond to standard DBT or other treatments.

Radically Open Dialectical Behavior Therapy (RO-DBT) was developed by Thomas Lynch, PhD as an evidence-based treatment for clients diagnosed with a range of disorders characterized by over-control. RO-DBT has proven to be an effective treatment for chronic depression, treatment-resistant anxiety, adult autism spectrum disorders, adult anorexia nervosa, and other control-centric personality disorders.

The aims of RO-DBT are to provide clients with greater receptivity and openness, flexible control, and intimacy and social connectedness.

Even if you choose to seek a deeper therapeutic modality such as EMDR or SE, both of which are discussed momentarily, or a combination of talk therapy and a deeper therapy, the process begins with a thorough evaluation of your background and your readiness to do the work involved in your process of healing. The evaluation may also include clinical testing to rule out or rule in certain diagnoses.

Bodywork

Because so many of a neglected person's thoughts, emotions, and behavioral reactions stem from the unconscious mind, I recommend doing bodywork as an adjunct to talk therapy. Bodywork accesses the deeper levels of your consciousness to help you heal. Bodywork stresses the body-mind connection, rather than the mind-body connection. It recognizes that we carry every memory on a cellular level in our bodies. There are many methods of bodywork, including touch methods like shiatsu, Rolfing, and Reiki, and non-touch methods like breathwork, Qigong, and Tai Chi.

Many of my clients say things like, "I know in my head what I am feeling is really not about what my partner (or boss or teacher or friend or coworker or kid) just said or did, but that's not how it feels in my body." Bodywork helps these clients sort out what's going on in the present versus the past.

Typically, these clients have already worked very hard to recognize what happened to them in childhood and understand what role they played in their family of origin. Moreover, they've discovered the strategy they used to counteract the neglect and/or abuse. Still, they suffer the after-effects of the lack of attachment they experienced as a child.

These clients benefit from bodywork because they understand the facts and strategies of what happened, and they can intellectualize that now is now and then was then. But they also still carry the feelings and emotions of the past, and these feelings and emotions from the past get triggered when a situation in the present feels (in any way) similar to what happened in the past.

Just talking about this fact doesn't seem to resolve it. A client can be in talk therapy for years and years and still suffer the ill effects of the past.

Some people, because one of their childhood survival strategies was to deny and minimize what was happening, may get angry at themselves whenever they have a feeling. They have great difficulty having compassion for the hurting child inside them who still cries, sobs, and gets angry and afraid when triggered. Telling such a client to be nice to the child inside who seems to them to be having a temper tantrum does not work. More is needed. Often, that "more" is provided by bodywork.

EMDR

EMDR (short for Eye Movement Desensitization and Reprocessing) is a well researched and effective form of psychotherapy where the individual is asked to recall and talk about distressing events while focusing on a bilateral sensory input (such as side-to-side eye movements or hand tapping. This technique has proven effective in treating serious trauma and Post-Traumatic Stress Disorder (PTSD). In addition, EMDR is used to treat a variety of other conditions including pain reduction, and addictions.

How the discovery of the effect of eye movements on trauma took place is fascinating. The method was discovered not by a clinical researcher working diligently in a university or a hospital laboratory, but by chance. In 1979, Francine Shapiro was working on a doctorate in English literature with only a side interest in psychology when she received a cancer diagnosis. At that point, her path radically changed. As she says in her book on EMDR, "When a potentially fatal disease strikes, it can be a watershed that marks a change in the course of one's life."[12]

After Francine's doctors pronounced that the cancer was no longer present but made no guarantees that it would not come back, she set out to find psychological and physiological methods to enhance physical health. She studied extensively and got her doctorate in clinical psychology.

In the spring of 1987, while walking in the park, Dr. Shapiro noticed that she was having disturbing thoughts. Upon paying close attention, she also noticed that they subsequently disappeared when her eyes began moving rapidly back and forth in an upward diagonal. This was the beginning of her research and the development of EMDR, which, as stated above, has proven to be effective in reducing reactions resulting from early-life trauma and PTSD.

Clients often ask me how and why EMDR works to reduce their suffering. I reply that I don't exactly understand why it works, and neither does anyone else, really, but they should just accept that it does work. According to the official explanation, EMDR seems to unlock the nervous system, allowing the brain to process the traumatic experience. That may also be what is happening in REM or dream sleep; the eye movements may help to process the unconscious material. But mostly this explanation is an informed guess about what's actually going on.

---

12 Shapiro, F. (2001). *Eye movement desensitization and reprocessing (EMDR): Basic principles, protocols, and procedures.* Guilford Press.

Somatic Experiencing

Somatic Experiencing (SE) is a body-oriented approach to healing trauma and other stress disorders. SE is the life's work of Dr. Peter A. Levine. The method results from his multidisciplinary study of stress physiology, psychology, ethology, biology, neuroscience, indigenous healing practices, and medical biophysics. Generally speaking, SE releases traumatic shock, which is key to transforming and resolving the wounds of developmental attachment trauma.

The SE approach is typically used when a person is stuck in the fight, flight, or freeze set of responses. For these individuals, SE provides clinical tools to resolve these fixated physiological states.

Mindfulness-Based Stress Reduction

Mindfulness-Based Stress Reduction (MBSR) is a structured pro-gram that teaches the practice of mindfulness in an effort to alleviate pain and improve physical and emotional well-being. The program was established by Jon Kabat-Zinn at the University of Massachusetts Medical School.

Mindfulness is the sustained, moment-to-moment awareness of phys-ical sensations, perceptions, affective states, imagery, and thoughts. It is the process of focusing attention to direct experience without judg-ment, comparison, or evaluation.

In MBSR, mindfulness is directly practiced in sitting and walking meditation, movement, and eating. Participants are taught techniques for bringing mindfulness and the associated benefits to all parts of their lives.

Two decades of published research indicate that people who complete an MBSR program report greater ability to cope more effectively with both short- and long-term stressful situations. By learning to actively participate in the management of health and well-being, many participants report they are better able to manage stress, fear, anger, anxiety, and depression both at home and in the workplace. Participants have also stated that they feel less judgmental and critical of themselves, and subsequently of others. Many report a decrease in the frequency and length of medical visits to hospitals and other professional health-care providers. There also is a noticeable decrease in the use of prescription and non-prescription medications.

Yoga

Today, yoga is considered a form of mindfulness training under the category of bodywork. The underlying purpose of all the aspects of the practice of yoga is to reunite the individual Self with the absolute of pure consciousness. In fact, the word "yoga" means literally "joining." Union with this unchanging reality liberates the spirit from all sense of separation, freeing it from the illusion of time, space, and causation. It is only our own ignorance, our inability to discriminate between the real and the unreal, that prevents us from realizing our true nature.

Today in the West there are many practices of yoga, each having a specific focus. For many people, yoga is simply a way to stretch and tone the muscles and strengthen the body. However, the benefits of yoga are far more than just movement and exercise. When used and practiced properly, yoga can be a valuable tool to connect you to your inner Self.

Other Options

The modalities listed above are but a few of the options offered by professional therapists to help neglected and abused people heal. Equine therapy, family sculpting, family of origin intensives, therapeutic massage, transformational breathwork, Integral Breath Therapy (IBT) and soul retrieval are names of a few of the other forms of alternative healing. Please see the Resources section at the end of the book for more suggestions of bodywork and grounding techniques.

Chapter 24
Play

Sometimes, neglected children were so busy trying to get the attention of their caregivers or attempting to behave in the impossible role of an adult that they didn't have any energy left over to play. Other times neglected children did play, but in the form of fantasy and pretend—making up a world in which they were safe and loved.

Typically, healthy play is something that happens spontaneously in children who are naturally creative and seek joy. Healthy play is the way children learn and use their vast imaginations to develop into healthy adults. If you did not have enough opportunities to play or your family's dysfunction was so egregious that you couldn't play at all, you may not now, as an adult, even know how to play.

Playing is a way to get to know your inner child. If you doubt that you have an inner child, think about why Disneyland and other amusement parks are so popular. These venues are for the children, yes, but they're also for the children inside all the adults. They're a chance to play.

If you struggle with play, I suggest you take a trip to the nearest toy store or the toy department of a large department store. Stay focused on your feelings as you wander the aisles. Was there a toy that you wanted as a child but never got? Was there a childhood activity that you never got to do? Make a note of the aha moments you get when you see a toy that sparks your interest.

For me, it was finger paints. My mother was a neat freak and wouldn't allow me to "get messy." When I got into recovery, I bought some finger paints and made a big mess. It was fun. My four-year-old was delighted. For you it may be flying a kite at the beach, playing with Legos, cuddling with a stuffed animal. Puzzles are fun as well.

Whatever calls to you, get it. If you have something in mind that the toy store doesn't have, chances are you can order it online. You deserve to let your inner child play. There's nothing silly or stupid about this. It is filling in one of the blanks that were denied you as a child. As you finally indulge in play, notice the joy that comes with it.

For those of you who have your own children, get down on the floor and let them teach you the joy of play. It's OK to act silly. Your actual children will benefit from your willingness to be with them and play as much as your inner child will benefit.

Chapter 25
Establishing Healthy Relationships (Intimate and Other)

Muriel came from a well-respected, wealthy family in which both parents were business professionals. She was tended by a nanny and only saw her parents as they came and went from work. Often, they were exhausted when they arrived home and had no time or energy left for their child.

Muriel's mother had returned to work when Muriel was 6 weeks old; therefore, her nanny was the only caregiver Muriel could remember having. The nanny, Margaret, had children of her own and lived on the property adjacent to Muriel's house. Sometimes Margaret would bring her own children with her to the "big house," as it was called. Muriel recognized right away that Margaret loved her children more than she loved Muriel. Early on, she understood that Margaret was not her real mother and could not love her as a real mother.

Muriel was given every opportunity and earthly possession, yet she lacked the one thing she wanted most – her mother and father's attention and nurturing. She wanted to be seen by them, but instead they were like wispy ghosts wafting in and out, up and down the stairs, speaking in hushed voices. She only had Margaret, who could not love her as much as she deserved, because caring for her was a job.

Muriel excelled in private school and was in classes for gifted students. She was also involved in music, playing the flute in the school orchestra. Her parents enrolled her in gymnastics, in which she also excelled. In fact, Muriel did well with practically everything she did. In this way, she hoped to make her parents proud and that they would notice she was being a good daughter.

And they were proud, but only so far as they could brag to their friends about how well Muriel was doing in all her activities. Margaret drove her to those activities and was also the one who attended her performances. Muriel's parents were too busy working. Under all her accomplishments and the praise, there still remained a nagging sense that she was not good enough and could do more.

Looking at this family from the outside, one would say the parents were doing a good job. They worked long hours so they could provide Muriel with all the educational opportunities and material things a child could want. And this is true. They were doing a good job providing in this sense. But they failed to really see Muriel and listen to her. They failed to get to know her and to spend quality time with her.

Muriel appreciated all the things she was given, but she needed more at her core. She was very lonely and felt there was no one with whom she could talk. She daydreamed of being tucked in each night and given hugs. And she blamed herself for her parents' inability to spend time with her.

When Muriel was a teenager, she began having bouts of depression, and that affected her grades. Her parents became concerned. She was placed on antidepressant medication, which helped stabilize her mood, and her grades returned to normal. Over the years and throughout college Muriel took a variety of medications to help with depression and anxiety.

She married a young man from a wealthy family like her own. He was a high achiever like herself. The wedding was large and elaborate. Muriel's husband, Roger, pursued a career in law and attained a position with a firm in a large city. Muriel got a job teaching music at a local private school.

Roger worked long hours. Although on medication, Muriel was still desperately lonely. She became part of a volunteer service organization and socialized in the community with women like herself.

As time went on, Roger and Muriel became more and more distant. He was short-tempered and aloof and seemed secretive. Muriel couldn't exactly pinpoint what was wrong or why she felt angry and sad at the same time, but she knew something had changed in their relationship.

Muriel enrolled in yoga classes. One evening, she arrived home from class early and found Roger looking at pornography on the computer. She said nothing, telling herself that all men do that. The next day, feeling suspicious, Muriel examined the history on his computer. She found that not only had he been looking at pornography, he had been chatting with other women and searching profiles for prostitutes.

Her level of devastation was beyond words. She confronted Roger, who at first denied what had been happening. Then, faced with Muriel's findings, he admitted that he had been looking at different women online but only because he was curious. Muriel wanted to believe him, but in her heart she knew there was more to the story.

When her pain became so great that she felt suicidal, Muriel reached out for help. She searched for a therapist who specialized in sex addiction (a CSAT) because she wanted to know if that was indeed what was happening with Roger.

In time, Roger also sought help with sexual compulsivity, because he could not stop his behaviors even when they violated his own sense of integrity. He went to a separate therapist and began to attend 12 step sexual recovery meetings and a men's therapy group.

For a while, it seemed that "recovery" was taking over their lives. However, both Muriel and Roger knew that recovery was the only way they could save themselves and their relationship.

In time, Muriel started doing work on her family of origin dys-function, learning that how she was raised was neglectful. She began to understand that because of her loneliness and desire for love, she had been vulnerable.

Roger had been raised by parents who only focused on material achievement and being seen as successful. The pressure had always been strong to do more, be more, and avoid any sign of weakness. Having feelings and talking about what he was experiencing emotionally were considered weakness. Through his own work, Roger learned that sex was the way he learned to shut down the constant critical voice in his head that reminded him that he was never enough.

The story of Muriel and Roger is not here to suggest that it is neglectful for both parents to have a career or even to hire a nanny to care for the child. The important point here is that there must be interaction and nurturing of the child when the parents are home. It is not the amount of time spent with the child, but the quality of that time.

SAFETY

Safety is connected to more than just watching your back when you are walking down a dark street in a dangerous neighborhood. For neglected children, even the home is not a safe situation because while there they don't get the attention they need to develop in healthy ways.

Through the developmental stages, the brain and body learn to recognize cues to know when someone or something is safe or not. But for many neglected children, this does not happen. Because their home is not safe, they never learn to distinguish between safe and unsafe people and situations. This portion of their emotional and psychological development just does not take place.

Because the neglected child (and later the adult) craves attention yet can't distinguish who is and who isn't safe, he or she may allow himself or herself to be taken advantage of by people who are not safe. This not only applies to sexual predators and con artists, but to people who subconsciously prey on vulnerable people in less obvious ways. Because the neglected child/adult is programmed to seek attention at any cost, abuse of some sort is often part of the picture of both their childhood and adult history. Therefore, the neglected/abused child becomes a neglected/abused adult.

The child/adult who was neglected by being so overly controlled that he or she didn't learn who he or she was or what he or she wanted might also have trouble picking a healthy partner. When a child is programmed to deny the Self and only obey orders, that person, as an adult, likely hasn't developed the skill of knowing what he or she likes or doesn't like, so, therefore, he or she does not have the ability to make a wise decision when choosing a partner. It's easier to take orders and be compliant than to make a decision based on Self. Being told what to do, including who to be with, feels comfortable and familiar to adults who were overly controlled as children because that is how they have been programmed.

As stated earlier, I believe neglect to be the foundation stone of outright abuse, although many neglected adults have developed ways of denying, justifying, and minimizing the abusive behavior they experience in relationships. They do this because they lack the discernment necessary to avoid unhealthy relationships. What they define as "safety" may be that they feel loved so they ignore all sorts of red flags—because attention and the feeling of pseudo-love created by attention (even abusive attention) are their most important foundational needs. Thus, when their relationship becomes toxic, they may employ every effort to fix it, not realizing that no one can change another person's behavior. Other people do not change unless they want to change.

When neglected and/or abused adults eventually get in touch with themselves and trust their intuition, they can develop the discernment necessary to detach from abusive relationships and to avoid unhealthy people. They can also begin to exude the positive energy needed to attract healthy adults into their lives.

Individuals neglected as children often get confused as to the meaning of love. And how could they not when they never saw it? Thus, they tend to become attracted to people who are not good for them. And negative Self-talk about the bad choices they make only adds to the pain.

Here is how this process develops in the unconscious part of the brain: The psyche in the developing child develops strategies for the child to get the attention he or she needs. Basically, the child finds ways in which to please his or her caregivers and to attract attention. The child is an energy sponge and keenly empathic. The child can read his or her caregivers and recognize any sign of emotional energy. The child then learns to either absorb and carry around that energy themselves or to deplete themselves of their child energy to help the adult. The child believes that he or she can fix whatever is wrong in the adult.

All of this is, of course, carried in the brain, waiting to surface in adult relationships.

When the child grows up and is ready to choose someone with whom to be in relationship, the same energy is used to recognize a partner. Very likely, the person to whom the now adult is attracted will have one or more of the same characteristics of his or her childhood caregivers. Because the caregivers were wounded in their own ways, the chosen adult partner will often have some form of inner wound-edness of his or her own. The inner Self of the adult is drawn to this and unrealistically believes that this damaged partner selection is "the one." Often, sex seals the deal. Or not.

SEX

There is often, especially if you have been neglected and deprived of real love, a tendency to get sex and love entangled and to have trouble telling the two things apart. Hot sex and real love can and should be deeply connected, yet they are vastly different. And often, they are not connected at all. This is a real conundrum for neglected individuals, especially in the beginning of a relationship.

Most wounded people get drawn into having sex way before they know what they are dealing with. The sexual component is a complex topic in and of itself. Suffice it to say that sex is a good thing—a natural human drive that can be pleasurable and mutually fulfilling—when one knows how to handle it. I compare it to fire, water, and other powerful elements of the universe. Fire can keep you warm, cook your food, light your way. It can also kill you, burn your house down, and make things explode. Water can keep your body hydrated, clean things, cool things off, boil food, and a myriad of other positive things. It can also flood, dampen, drown, wash away soil through erosion, and kill. So, we must admit that the powers of our world have polar opposites—positives and negatives. When used as they were meant to be used, they can enhance our lives and be life-giving. When used carelessly, they can be destructive.

Sex is a power that was meant primarily to help us propagate. Because we need to propagate to perpetuate the species, our brains are pro-grammed to experience sex as a pleasurable and a life-enhancing experience. It is supposed to be pleasurable, relaxing, and enjoyable, and because of that, we are likely to have sex often enough to ensure the survival of our species.

When sex is used for reasons other than procreation and/or enhancing an already good relationship, it is not the deep experience of intimacy that it was meant to be. When the relationship is vibrant, both parties are fully emotionally present, having fun, and feeling no guilt or embarrassment.

Unfortunately, rather than following the natural flow of sharing each other's bodies in an equal relationship, sex is often used to control and manipulate, to demonstrate power-over, to act out rage, or to relieve tension. Granted, sex does relieve tension. But when it is a purely mechanical experience, there is something missing.

When you are awake and aware of what you are doing, you will understand how important it is to learn how to use the power of sex in a healthy way, where nothing is missing from the experience.

Sex is and has been one of the most controversial topics on the world's stage. Is it only right and permissible for sex to occur inside a relationship between a married man and woman? Reality tells us differently. Today we know that human sexuality is far more complex than the narrow moral definition that society (and the church) formerly held.

Another oft-asked question is: When is sex problematic? I believe the answer to that lies in the intention for being sexual. When one person uses another person strictly for personal gratification, he or she is making the other an object. An object is a *thing* to be used for one's own pleasure without regard for the other's humanity. This practice dehumanizes both parties.

Yet another common question is: Must there be love? Clearly, plenty of people have sex without being in love, and they are perfectly OK with that. As far as I'm concerned, that's fine. I pass no judgment on casual sex. Sex and love are not the same thing, and they can healthfully be separated by consenting adults. That said, I think the presence of at least mutual respect and admiration and a mutual decision to be sexual is the minimum prerequisite for healthy expression of one's sexuality.

One way to start understanding the power of sex is by learning to relate to our bodies. In the past, our bodies were considered our enemy (the flesh). Now, even in spiritual and religious circles, we are recognizing that our bodies are magnificent creations for which to be thankful as part of the whole of who we are.

Still, shame is associated with certain parts of our bodies. Our brains, hearts, hands, eyes, noses, mouths, and teeth are OK to take care of and a reason for which to be thankful. But other parts of our bodies are often objects of ridicule and shame. Just the fact that parents named them different names or never talked about them indicates that these parts of our body are shameful. Crude jokes abound regarding these body parts. Yet, they are each deserving of respect, as are all the rest of the parts of the body. And even though regard for these parts of our bodies has been repressed, the sex drive that is a natural part of our creation still remains.

We must accept that lust is a powerful emotion so we can learn to recognize it when we feel it and make a conscious decision about what to do with it. When the natural emotion of lust is felt, shame often accompanies it. When this happens, healthy curiosity and arousal become secretive.

Shame provides the perfect opportunity for the secretive practice of viewing pornography, which distorts healthy sexuality and uses artificial means to produce high-intensity arousal. On January 20, 2015, it was reported on NBC Business News that the pornography industry pulls in over ninety-seven billion dollars annually. I quote, "Globally, porn is a $97 billion industry, according to Kassia Wosick, assistant professor of sociology at New Mexico State University. At present between $10 and $12 of that comes from the United States."[13] In Japan, it has been reported that the birth rate is down due, in part, to so many people artificially meeting their sexual needs through pornography rather than through a real relationship.[14] So is porn the social evil that some people think it is? Probably not. The problem is not pornography, it's the shame we attach to it.

If you can admit that what you are experiencing is lust, that's great. As long as you know what you are feeling, you can make an informed decision. But, at least for now, please do not call it love. Lust is a perfectly fine human emotion, but it, alone, is not love. Lust is part of being human, but you have to be the one in control of it; otherwise, it will control you. Lust will make you think that it is love, thus keeping you stuck in a whirlwind of unfulfilling relationships that may be counter to what you are really looking for.

When I ask clients how they learned about sex, the answer is usually that they learned from pornography, from older brothers and sisters, from other kids, and from parents/teachers who just gave them the

---

13 Morris, C. (2015). Things are looking up in America's porn industry. *NBC News*. Retrieved from https://www.nbcnews.com/business/business-news/things-are-looking-americas-porn-industry-n289431.

14 Brook, B. (2017). Japan's Population is Shrinking Because No One is Having Sex. *NY Post*. Retrieved from https://nypost.com/2017/07/10/japans-population-is-shrinking-because-no-one-is-having-sex/.

physical facts of growing up with no discussion of psychology or emotions. Other times they say they had to learn about sex on their own. All of these responses indicate to me that too many of us carry shame and taboo attitudes about sexuality, so much so that we have trouble giving positive knowledge to our offspring.

Nevertheless, Western society is one of the most highly sexualized cultures on Earth. Sexual advertisements and innuendoes are everywhere. We are given extremely mixed messages. On the one hand, we are supposed to be highly sexual; on the other hand, we are supposed to be ashamed of our sexuality.

We need to stop feeling ashamed of our bodies and our natural urges. We need to realize that sex does not equal love. We need to understand that sex is powerful, and it can be a wonderful, pleasurable experience when we make the conscious decision about when, how, and with whom we want to share our bodies. We also need to understand that having sex for the wrong reasons can be harmful to ourselves and our partners.

COUPLES' WORK

Often, people consider seeking outside help in the form of therapy because of problems in their intimate relationship. This may manifest in many ways. Usually, therapy starts with couples' work, that is, if the partner is willing to go. When I hear most often from clients is things like:

- "We have been together X number of years. At first, I felt so in love with him/her. I'm not sure what happened because now, although I still love him/her, I am not *in love* anymore."

- "When we were dating, sex was wonderful and exciting. As soon as the wedding was over, though, he/she changed. I felt so disappointed on the honeymoon, but I didn't say anything. Now we haven't had sex in a year."
- "Everyone thinks we are the perfect family. If they only knew. He/she is charming and helpful to everyone else. He/she is active in the church, socially fun in public, yet at home he/she is sullen and mean-spirited. He/she makes hurtful remarks to me. I feel like now we are just friends and our marriage is more like a business transaction."
- "He/she is a great parent, but unfaithful to me. He/she is more interested in the computer than me."
- "He/she he has let himself/herself go, complaining all the time, spending all the money. It's hopeless."

All of these reasons for coming to therapy are really about the same thing. Each member of the couple is wounded and hurting, yet neither is emotionally intimate enough with their partner to turn to their partner for help.

Without going into a whole explanation of couples' dynamics, suffice it to say that in most cases, neither partner has gone within and done the deep work of resolving his or her own wounding, and therefore has not discovered why the couple was attracted to one another in the first place.

As discussed above, there are reasons that people are attracted to others with some of the same traits as their childhood caregivers. Those reasons are because that is what is familiar, and because their inner child needs the experience so it can heal and grow up. The human psyche seeks health any way it can get it.

The short answer to this "damaged partner dilemma" is to heal yourself first, and that comes about by getting to know yourself. Start with what really happened in childhood and discover what strategy (pattern) your psyche adopted for you in order to survive. Once you know that, you can learn to pay attention to when you are triggered and why. You can ask: What is the emotion that you feel, does it feel familiar, does it remind you of something that happened when you were a child? Know what is happening in you. That awareness is the first step in changing it.

Even if you don't know how to recognize real love when you feel it, you can learn now. You can begin by loving yourself first. Accept that no matter how hard you try, you are going to make mistakes. As Pia Mellody teaches, the number one universal fact about humans is that, even though humans are imperfect, each person is valuable. Regardless of what you do or have done, you have inherent worth and you are worthy of love.

When each member of the couple is committed to working out the broken ways in which they relate, couples' therapy can work wonders. In doing couples' work, the focus is not on one or the other person, but on recognizing and fixing the unhealthy interaction between the two individuals. There are many fine modalities for couples' work—each capable of producing amazing results when both parties are willing to be honest with themselves and each other and are open to looking within. Loving kindness, active listening, and understanding become some of the foundational pieces for rebuilding what was broken.

Chapter 26
Setting a Foundation Using Boundaries

One way to begin living in balance is learning to set appropriate boundaries with others. As a neglected person, it's likely that your family of origin was boundaryless. Thus, as an adult, you don't know much if anything at all about having healthy emotional and psychological boundaries. As a child, you didn't know you could say no to something or someone in an appropriate way.

When neglected individuals are first introduced to the concept of boundaries, they may carry it to an extreme of being walled in or walled off. *Everything* becomes a boundary.

The purpose of a healthy boundary is to respect your inner Self, to request what you need in order to feel safe and comfortable in your own skin. Since you are designed to be in relationships (whether intimate or not), you'd best learn how to negotiate what you want and need so you can feel a sense of value while not devaluing the other.

To explain boundaries, I will use the method taught by Pia Mellody in her Post Induction Training (now known as "The Meadows Model") on family of origin trauma on the way to becoming a "functional adult."[15] I believe Pia's teaching on boundaries is clear and concise and promotes intimacy in the relationship.

PHYSICAL AND SEXUAL BOUNDARIES

Physical and sexual boundaries are boundaries that protect and contain the body. When someone stands too close, you can step back. This is protecting your personal space. When you notice someone leaning away from you or stepping back, it is a signal to you that you are too close to them and you can move away yourself. This is called containing yourself.

As you think about physical boundaries, take into account the fact that other cultures and individuals may differ in what is comfortable physical space. You have to determine what is comfortable for you. The other person may not mean to invade your space, or they may. Whichever is the case, you have the right to move away. If that does not work, you may respectfully state that you are uncomfortable and ask for what you need.

The same goes for hugging. Many people, because of something that happened in their past, are not comfortable being touched. You have a right to say that you do not feel comfortable being touched in a certain way. Similarly, it is best to ask if the other person wants a hug or is comfortable being touched before giving a hug. This is especially true in today's current #MeToo society.

---

15 Mellody, P., (2003). Post Induction Therapy Workshop, Boundaries Unit II, Wickenburg, AZ (pp. 10-21).

I am extremely happy that, at last, victims of sexual assault and harassment (male and female) are coming out into the open. However, the perception of what is assault and harassment is so subjective that a behavior you may consider innocent may be taken the wrong way. That's why it's best to ask before acting.

You also have the right to set boundaries around being sexual with someone. You have the right to say yes or no without being peppered with numerous questions. You have the right to not be coerced into doing anything you do not want to do.

By the way, "being sexual" involves a lot more than just sexual intercourse. Flirting, kissing, engaging in sexual banter, touching, foreplay, mutual masturbation: all of these count as "being sexual." And you have the right to determine when, with whom, and how you will be sexual. This is a very important and intimate boundary.

In earlier decades, women were taught that it was their duty to give themselves sexually to their partners even though they may not have wanted sex for whatever reason. Hopefully, times have changed.

It is important that couples openly, frankly, and kindly speak to one another about what brings them pleasure during sex. This may take some inner work where each individual is able to determine what he or she likes. The assumption is that the couple is connected intimately on an emotional level so the sexual relationship can be a full experience with each member emotionally present. In so doing, it is important that each partner respect the boundaries of the other.

THE TALKING AND LISTENING BOUNDARY

Verbal and non-verbal communication requires boundaries as well. In preparing how to present yourself verbally, it is important to first go inside and examine your thoughts. Pausing in this way is especially necessary if the topic you want to discuss is something over which you and the other person disagree or feel strong emotions.

There may be a triggering event that causes you to have a thought or an assumption and then an emotion that goes with the thought or assumption. It is easy at this point to let fly with words that match your strong emotion. Your thought or assumption may cause you to "make up a story" to go with the trigger, and that story that may or may not be true. When you let your angry inner child (usually a teenager) handle the trigger in this way, you are reacting rather than remaining in the driver's seat of your life's bus.

The goal here is to handle the situation in a more balanced way. This may be difficult to do until you become practiced at it. More than likely, accusations and expressions of anger lead you into conflict and resentment rather than what you really want, which is to understand the other person and to be relational. Angry outbursts, sarcasm, blaming, and shaming words are counterproductive and show lack of containment. Strive to speak frankly but respectfully to the other person, as you would like to be spoken to.

The other extreme when you are triggered is to stuff your emotions. Many neglected people do this, because this is the strategy they learned in childhood. However, acting as if something didn't bother you, denying reality, making up a story to justify what happened, or just numbing out doesn't work in the long run. Stuffing feelings doesn't make them go away. Those feelings will end up coming out sideways, often in the form of an overreaction to something rather insignificant.

Why do neglected people do this? Not feeling like you have the right to question, to have an opinion, to know the truth, and to get attention is part of it. As a neglected child, you learned not to "make waves" because the result from your primary caregivers would be a scary display of emotion, hurtful comments, no reaction at all, or something even worse. Thus, the lesson of keeping quiet and stuffing your emotions.

Sometimes when children try asking questions or having an opinion that differs from their caregivers, they are labeled as a bad kid. And over time this label can become a reality. Children will get attention any way they can get it, so scapegoating is the way these children get it. Whether too controlled (stuffing feelings) or out of control (scape-goating behavior), both are extremes.

The balanced way is to slow down and look inside yourself first. To do this, you must first notice when you are triggered. Usually triggers come with a whoosh that feels like an energy rush accompanied by thoughts and emotions. This is when you have a chance to change your behavior, but you have to catch the trigger when it happens and before you are already reacting.

When you do catch yourself being triggered, ask yourself, "What is happening? Am I assuming something that is not necessarily true? Am I confused?" If you can, ask the other person to clarify what he or she is saying, or to explain what just happened. A non-confrontational statement might be, "I'm not clear about what you just said. Can you tell me more? I want to understand what you really mean." This is a method for containing yourself in a two-way conversation.

Let's think about what it is like to care for yourself in listening to the other person. It is really all about the energy in the room. When someone says something to you that is not true or is hurtful, blaming, or shaming, or which is triggering to your inner Self, you have a right to protect yourself energetically. You have a right to set a listening boundary.

Pia Mellody describes the listening boundary as like holding a catcher's mitt with a giant funnel in front it. Before letting the words into your inner Self, imagine them sliding through the funnel into your catcher's mitt first. Then you can silently ask yourself, "Is this true, or is this not true? Do I need more information?" If the words are true, you can permit them to enter your inner Self. If they are not, you can respectfully disagree with what has been said.

By the way, this doesn't give you the right to throw back insults. Remember, you are attempting to be known and to know the other person. If his or her words require more information, you can ask questions. The idea is to come from a place of being empowered and having respect for your precious inner Self, while also having respect for the other person.

It is important to understand that boundaries are requests, so they may not always be respected. However, it is empowering just to be able to set them. If you were neglected as a child, this may be the first time you have clearly set a boundary to take care of yourself, rather than taking everything in and being hurt, angry, and sad. Therefore, congratulate yourself. Here are some things you can do if you and your partner are not getting along and you're struggling to maintain balance:

- You can take a break.
- You can state, "You may be right. Let me sit with that and get back to you."

- You can say, "Help me understand why you feel that way."
- Stick with "I" statements, saying what you need to feel safe in the relationship.
- Seek the help of a professional couples' therapist. Almost always, it's not one or the other of you but the "dance" you do together that is the problem. Most couples fight about the same thing over and over, like the same old tired script of a bad play. A therapist can coach you to break the pattern and get underneath what is really going on.
- Increase your own Self-care. This is vital to your process of healing and helps you navigate the challenges of changing your childhood survival strategies to adult interactions with Self and others.

Please see the resources section for good books on setting appropriate boundaries.

Chapter 27
Understanding Love and Respect

When you are caring for your physical needs through sensible eating and exercise and when a sense of safety is established, you are no longer neglecting yourself. You realize you are inherently worthy of love and belonging. This is greatly empowering.

Let's look at what love and respect really are. We'll start with love. There are so many definitions and variations of 'love' that it can become confusing, especially if you didn't see it or have it modeled for you as a child. Here are some things to consider:

- **Unconditional love:** Children are deserving of unconditional love because they are children and they are learning how to be in this world. Therefore, parents, though they may be highly frustrated by their child's misbehavior, are required to love their children anyway and guide them to correct behavior. Need I say that parenting done right is an enormous responsibility? Parents do and will mess up because they are themselves human, but they always return to gathering their child/children up and saying, for example, "I was very tired yesterday when you spilled soup all over the carpet, and I overreacted. I am sorry for that and I love you."

- **Conditional love:** Adults cannot expect unconditional love from another adult. They are adults and the assumption is that they have learned developmentally how to be a functional adult. The problem arises when the adult was neglected and did not learn that. Therefore, when adults make mistakes, a neglected person may not know how to respond in a relationship. Generally, they go to what worked in the past, which may not work in adult life. Then, the person tends to either get into unhealthy relationships over and over, go through a series of breakups, or stay in a relationship that is abusive.

  Neglected, vulnerable people often look to others to meet their emotional needs. This practice is often referred to as the "vending machine philosophy." When you use a vending machine, you pick out what you want, put your money in the slot, and out comes exactly what you want. However, this idea can't be used on humans because humans are not machines. We have to learn to take care of ourselves. We may have set boundaries to make us feel safe, but the other has the right to say "no." Sometimes people who say "yes" are not being completely honest, but they will agree initially, then use excuses later as to why they did not follow through with what they said they would do or not do. Either way, it is not realistic to expect another adult to meet all your needs.

Let's look at the idea of respect as it applies to love. Actually, you can't have real love without respect. What exactly defines "respect." Respect means giving the other person space, both literally and emotionally. Respect means having regard for "otherness." When you have respect for others, you accept that not everyone else thinks like you and you let that be. Respect means letting go of outcomes.

If the other person chooses to do something in your intimate relationship or friendship that you don't like, then you get to decide how you are going to respond to that. You can: 1) let it go; 2) state your needs and feelings in a respectful way; 3) wait and trust you will know in time; or 4) leave the relationship. The most important part for you is considering what you now know and what is the decision that is best for you in the long run. Please remember that "no decision at all right now" is a valid decision. If you are in touch with your inner Self, you will know what to do and when to do it. Also consider checking your decision out with your trusted group or a therapist.

Respect also means setting boundaries to make yourself feel safe and to contain yourself by respecting the others' boundaries. All of this requires trust, trust for yourself and who you now know yourself to be and trust that the other person will not harm you. Trust is the foundation stone of a relationship. Once it is broken, it takes a long time and a lot of work to rebuild.

Love and respect go together and go in both directions, from the other person to you and from you to the other person.

Chapter 28
Think Universally

The Summer Day
by Mary Oliver

Who made the world?
Who made the swan, and the black bear?
This grasshopper, I mean
The one who has flung herself out of the grass
The one who is eating sugar out of my hand,
Who is moving her jaws back and forth instead of up and down-
Who is gazing around with her enormous and complicated eyes.
Now she lifts her pale forearms and thoroughly washes her face.
Now she snaps her wings open, and floats away.
I don't know exactly what a prayer is.
I do know how to pay attention, how to fall down
Into the grass, how to kneel down in the grass,
How to be idle and blessed, how to stroll through the fields,
Which is what I have been doing all day.
Tell me, what else should I have done?
Doesn't everything die at last, and too soon?
Tell me, what is it you plan to do
With your one wild and precious life?

NATURE

When I treat clients for neglect and trauma, I ask them to think of and describe a safe place—one in which they can go to feel relaxed, safe, and at home. Some clients had such horrendous childhoods that they can think of no place in which they feel safe. In such cases, I ask them to imagine a place, and we create the space in the therapy room for them to go to in their mind when they feel overwhelmed while processing a disturbing event.

Nine times out of ten they go to a scene that involves nature. Many people picture themselves at the seashore, sitting or lying on the clean white sand, gazing out at the ocean, and listening to the steady rhythm of the waves. Others go outside on a clear cool night outside of the city and look up at the millions of stars dotting the sky. Still others lie down in the grass, as Mary Oliver did on a summer's day, and study the creatures there.

There is something primordial and healing about nature. There is something in us that can let go in nature and relax into the timeless space of a natural environment.

SACRED MYSTERY

Often, when clients enter recovery they have tremendous problems with Step 3, which asks them to make a decision to turn their will and their life over to the care of the God of their understanding. Some people assume that this step is associated with going to church, reading the Bible or some other religious book, or accepting a dogma that doesn't fit for them or a God that is judging, punishing, or absent.

I ask them to throw all that away and to consider when, if at any time, they felt a sense of awe and were grateful just to be alive. Once again, their reply often has something to do with nature. Remember that this step says *the God of their understanding.* That can be unique for each person. If the only God of their understanding is the theocratic god, the one who keeps score of all their "sins" and punishes them accordingly, I tell them that they need to rethink that. I ask them to give themselves a break. I tell them they can create a Higher Power that resonates with who they are.

That is the challenge, isn't it? To discover Who We Are. As humans, we tend to want to understand and try to wrap our heads around the concept of a Higher Power. Throughout history, the concept of sacred mystery has often been formed into iconic visual representations that resemble ourselves, but with superpowers and human-like yet divine personalities.

Can't we just accept that some things are beyond human comprehension?

When we feel challenged with the idea that there is a something or someone that is capable of assisting us in our healing, we can picture the NASA satellite photograph of the cosmos and Earth's tiny place in it. There is so much we do not know. With all you are doing to become whole, we can trust that love and kindness are at the root of whatever it is that is guiding and helping us. And that can be enough.

Part Five
Moving Forward as You Progress in Your Healing

"If you want to awaken all of humanity, then awaken all of yourself. If you want to eliminate the suffering in the world, then eliminate all that is dark and negative in yourself. Truly, the greatest gift you have to give is that of your own self-transformation."

Lao Tzu

Chapter 29
The Destination/Transformation

A popular saying in the 1960s was, "Today is the first day of the rest of your life." But what does this quote really mean? To me, it means life flows one day at a time. It is never too late and you are never too old or too damaged to begin living the life you want. Moreover, this quote suggests there will never be a time when you have "arrived." There is no destination. There is only this delight in each and every day and the gratitude of living your life, your way.

You are given a body. Your true Self lives within it. It knows, intuitively, right from wrong. It is your inner guidance system. You may not have been given the examples or the tools to know consciously that you are precious yet imperfect. You may not have been given the tools to live according to your inner guidance system, but you can reach out, get support, and learn. You may not feel worthwhile, abundant, and happy. But whether you feel these things in the beginning or not, you can reach the point where you do.

At the beginning of your life, you have a huge bank account and a period of time on the Earth. You may have spent a lot of your precious time just trying to survive what you did not get as a child. You don't have to do that anymore. You know now that you can choose. Changing and living differently is not easy or swift. But it happens every day to formerly neglected and overly controlled humans. You find your own reality.

When you have done your work, what will be different? When you have done your work, will you forget the neglect and the incidents that caused you pain as a child? When you have done your work, will you pick healthy partners and live happily ever after? What will make it worth it if these things do not happen?

In my experience, here is what is realistic.

When you have done the work of transformation (and that is what it is), you will be able to recognize patterns that are true for you. No one can do this work for you. Because you were not parented in a healthy way, it has now become your task to parent yourself. You now can get into the driver's seat of your life and learn how to let go of things you cannot control and how to control the things you can, and you can know the difference between the two.

You will probably never forget the incidents that hurt you and caused you to feel the emptiness inside. The upside is that you will not have the impactful emotions attached to the memories. You will be able to let go. Sometimes you will be triggered by something that comes up in the now that wakes up the amygdala and causes you emotional reactivity. The difference, after the work of transformation, is that you will be able to stop and ask, "What is this *really* about?" You will be able to catch yourself before your behavior kicks in and causes you pain in the now. You will be able to pause and go within, taking care of your activated inner child and say to that child, "I know you are hurting about that thing that happened in the past. I understand why that was so painful then. But now I am all grown up and this is not the same thing, although it feels the same. You can just relax and be a little child and I will take care of this. You are safe now. From now on, I (the adult Self) will be here to take care of you."

When you have done that, then you can take action to handle the trigger. Some of the healthy things you can do are:

- Call a trusted friend and talk about it.
- Set a boundary with the person who activated the trigger.
- Write about it in your journal.
- Talk to your Higher Power about it.
- Meditate.
- Go to a support group meeting and talk about it.
- Walk outside in nature and breathe deeply.
- Call your therapist and talk and/or set an appointment.
- Affirm yourself that you are precious and perfectly imperfect. (In fact, you should always do this when you feel triggered.)
- Sit very still in silence in a private place.
- Do bilateral tapping on yourself. For a further explanation, see EMDR or "bilateral stimulation."
- Do some kind of physical exercise. Move your body.
- Do any healthy activity that helps the emotions and reactivity to pass.
- Breathe. Concentrate on your breath and the present moment.

There is an energy to life. Before, you were carrying the negative energy of your past, and your unhealthy thinking patterns were manifestations of that energy. In becoming empowered and getting healthy, you are entering a phase in which you are starting to carry positive energy both inside and out.

I believe that when you get rid of the negative energy, you will begin to attract, like a magnet, healthier people. If you begin to hang out

with positive, healthier people, you will then attract healthier partners. Since you are now awake, you will be able to recognize what I
call big red flags and you will not ignore, justify, or minimize them like
you did in the past. When you find you are able to eliminate potential friends and partners based on your empowered, positive sense of
Self-worth, instead of just trying to satisfy the desperate wounding
inside yourself, you will find what you are looking for. Just make sure
you know what you are looking for and don't settle for anything less.

This process may take a while, but aren't you worth it? When you
have done your work, you will be able to tolerate being alone. You will
enjoy your own company. Accept that you are a work in progress, and
you will make progress through the work.

Chapter 30
Symbols

THE ETERNAL KNOT

Life is comprised of ups and downs. When things are going well, savor each moment. When things are not going well, know that this is part of life and not necessarily a personal punishment. One of the symbolic representations of this concept of life is the Eternal Knot.

I first saw the eternal knot when I was new in private practice and going through a very painful time in my personal life. I had started the new behavior of taking care of myself instead of everyone else, and I had scheduled a massage.

On the wall of the massage therapist's office, I spied a wooden replica of the eternal knot. It called to me. Somehow it held meaning for me. I followed the feeling I was having and asked what it was. The massage therapist said it was the Eternal Knot. I then looked it up, and the meaning of it captured me as well. So, subsequently, the knot became my logo.

Here is the meaning: The Eternal Knot is one of the eight auspicious signs of Tibetan Buddhism. It means the unity of wisdom and infinite compassion. Over the years, I have found this symbol to be greatly applicable to the struggle we all face to be fully human, awake, and empowered. Though similar to the Celtic Knot, it has a form all its own, thus giving us a visual representation of life as it is.

Although my clients come in with every conceivable problem, they really are all the same—wounded. All human beings desire to be loved and accepted and to feel that they belong. This, in Maslow's Hierarchy, is called Self-actualization.

Self-help work is slippery. Just when we think we have "arrived," we have a bad day and think we are back where we started. However, this is not so. When we consider that humans are a microcosm of the cosmos, there is a spiral nature to Self-actualization. Although we feel we are starting again, when we can visualize the cyclical nature of life, we see that we have simply come full circle. But we are at a higher level and, therefore, a higher understanding of who we are. We are aware of what is happening to us on the inside faster, and we can remedy the situation sooner, rather than suffering and following through with negative thoughts, feelings, and actions that make life even more miserable.

OTHER SYMBOLS WHICH MAY HOLD MEANING FOR YOU

There are many symbols which serve to wake us up to what is real and present. Which ones, if any, call to you?

The Christian Cross is seen as a representation of the instrument of the crucifixion of Jesus Christ.*

The OM is a sacred sound and spiritual symbol in Hinduism that signifies the essence of the ultimate reality and consciousness of Atman.*

The Star of David, known in Hebrew as the Shield of David, or Magen David, is a generally recognized symbol of modern Jewish identity and Judaism.*

The Tree of Life is a widespread archetype in the world's mythologies, related to the concept of the sacred tree more generally, hence in religious and philosophical tradition.

The Tree of Knowledge, connecting to heaven and the underworld and the Tree of Life, connecting all forms of creation, are both forms of the world tree or the cosmic tree. They are portrayed in various religions and philosophies as the same tree.*

*Source: www.wikipedia.org

Conclusion
The Wheels on the Bus—
A Metaphor for Life

You may have noticed that in several spots throughout this book I have talked about "getting into the driver's seat of your own bus." I have taken this concept from my colleague, Dr. Mary Pratt, who adapted it from one of the first songs I learned in Kindergarten, "The Wheels on the Bus."

When examined from the perspective of a metaphor, this song has quite a few messages for us. Although I have commented on each verse, know that if you view this simple little song in its entirety as metaphor, you will see the deeper meaning of it and how that relates to our lives.

For me, there is only one guideline for driving the bus:

My adult Self must remain in the driver's seat at all times even when I feel overwhelmed. Sometimes I may realize I have given up my driver's seat to another, either my inner child or someone outside myself. As soon as I realize this, I can get back in the seat of control, always recognizing my inherent worth.

THE WHEELS ON THE BUS

1. **Life goes on.**
   The wheels on the bus go round and round,
   round and round,
   round and round.
   The wheels on the bus go round and round,
   all around the town.

2. **Sometimes it rains.**
   The wipers on the bus go Swish, swish, swish;
   Swish, swish, swish;
   Swish, swish, swish.
   The wipers on the bus go Swish, swish, swish,
   all around the town.

3. **Sometimes you have to use your horn (voice).**
   The horn on the bus goes Beep, beep, beep;
   Beep, beep, beep;
   Beep, beep, beep.
   The horn on the bus go Beep, beep, beep,
   all around the town

4. **Our inner children are always inside us, chattering away**
   The children on the bus go Chatter, chatter, chatter;
   Chatter, chatter, chatter;
   Chatter, chatter, chatter.
   The children on the bus go Chatter, chatter, chatter,
   all around the town.

5. **Sometimes our inner babies get activated.**
    The babies on the bus say Wah, wah, wah;
    Wah, wah, wah;
    Wah, wah, wah.
    The babies on the bus say Wah, wah, wah,
    all around the town.

6. **Our inner negative voice wants our wounded inner baby to be quiet. This means we now become real parents to our inner child and not just "shush" it up.**
    The mommies on the bus say Shush, shush, shush;
    Shush, shush, shush;
    Shush, shush, shush.
    The mommies on the bus say Shush, shush, shush,
    all around the town.

7. **This is indicative of life. Just when we think we have it all together, here comes something else. We go up and then down, but the good news is, we can now get back up.**
    The people on the bus go Up and down,
    Up and down,
    Up and down.
    The people on the bus go Up and down,
    all around the town.

8. **A reminder of the ebb and flow of wealth and abundance in the form of money and our relationship to it.**
    The money on the bus goes, Clink, clink, clink;
    Clink, clink, clink;
    Clink, clink, clink.
    The money on the bus goes, Clink, clink, clink,
    all around the town.

9. When your inner child moves toward the front to get into the driver's seat, your adult Self, as the driver, kindly tells the child to take a seat behind you. There is great power and responsibility in being the bus driver of your own life.
   The driver on the bus says, Move on back,
   Move on back,
   Move on back;
   The Driver on the bus says, Move on back,
   all around the town.

Have a good journey!

Resources Using
Body Awareness Techniques

Eye Movement Desensitization and Reprocessing (EMDR)
www.emdria.org
866-451-5200

Somatic Experiencing (SE)
www.traumahealing.org
303-652-4035

Sensorimotor Psychotherapy
www.sensorimotorpsychotherapy.org
800-860-9258

For a list of therapists trained by Pia Mellody in Post Induction Therapy go to:
www.healingtraumanetwork.net
781-777-1172

Equine Assisted Therapy
www.pathintl.org
www.eagala.org

Jon Taylor, LCSW, CSAT, CMAT (uses neurofeedback, mindfulness, trauma informed yoga in addition to traditional psychotherapy)
jtaylortherapy@gmail.com
www.healingpathsrecovery.com

Stephen Levine, PhD. (uses yoga, Integral Breath Therapy 'IBT')
P.O. Box 5273
Salt Springs, FL 32134
kamilasdad@gmail.com
(licensed in Pennsylvania and Florida)

Dr. Mari Richko (Uses Asian bodywork)
www.centerforauthenticliving.biz

Transformational Breathing (non clinical)
www.transformationalbreath.com
Dr. Judith Kravitz

Mari A. Lee, LMFT, CSAT-S
www.growthcounselingservices.com
(uses "The Whale Pod" breathing technique, guided imagery, breathwork and Tai-Chi in addition to traditional psychotherapy)

Sherry Young, PhD, CSAT
www.rightfitconsulting.com
Suggested use of knitting, crocheting, needlework at home as grounding exercises

Radically Open Dialectical Behavior Therapy
www.radicallyopen.net
Thomas R. Lynch PhD.
  www.DaringVentures.com Carol Ann Ross, LMSW, CSAT, CMAT

Dialectical Behavior Therapy
https://behavioraltech.org/resources/faqs/
dialectical-behavior-therapy-dbt
Marsha Linehan PhD.

Neurofeedback
www.eeginfo.com/what-is-neurofeedback.jsp

Trauma Informed Yoga
www.eomega.org/article/what-is-trauma-informed-yoga

Mindfulness Based Relapse Prevention (MBRP)
http://www.mindfulrp.com

Integral Breath Therapy (IBT)
https://integrationconcepts.net/about/

Twelve Step Support
Group Information

Adult Children of Alcoholics/Dysfunctional Families
http://information@acawso.org
310-534-1815

Alcoholics Anonymous World Services, Inc.
PO Box 459
Grand Central Station
New York, NY 10017
212-870-3400
http://aa.org

Debtors Anonymous
P.O. Box 20322
New York, NY 10025-9992
http://debtorsanonymous.org

Gamblers Anonymous
National Service Office
P.O. Box 17173
Los Angeles, CA 90017
213-386-8789
http://gamblersanonymous.org/ga

Infidelity Survivors Anonymous
http://isurvivors.org

Narcotics Anonymous
World Service Office
P.O. Box 9999
Van Nuys, CA 91409
818-773-9999
http://na.org

Overeaters Anonymous
6075 Zenith Court
Rio Rancho, NM 87174
505-891-2664
http://oa.org

Recovering Couples Anonymous
15 Sea Bridge Way
Alameda, CA 94502
877-663-2317
http://info@recoveringcouples.org

Sex Addicts Anonymous
http://saa-recovery.org

Sexual Compulsives Anonymous
http://sca-recovery.org

Sex and Love Addicts Anonymous
http://slaafws.org/meetings

Underearners Anonymous
http://underearnersanonymous.org

*Disclaimer: Please know these resources are for informational purposes only and are not necessarily endorsed by the author. You, as the reader, have the choice of whether or not they are for you.

Suggested Reading

Adams, K. & Morgan, A. *When He's Married to Mom: How to Help Mother-Enmeshed Men Open Their Hearts to True Love and Commitment.* New York, NY: Fireside, 2007.

Brown, B. *I Thought It Was Just Me.* New York, NY: Gotham Books, 2007.

Brown, B. *Daring Greatly.* New York, NY: Gotham Books, 2012

Brown, B. *The Gifts of Imperfection.* New York, NY: Gotham Books, 2010.

Brown, B. *Rising Strong.* New York: Spiegel & Grau, 2015.

Carnes, P. *The Betrayal Bond: Breaking Free of Exploitive Relationships.* Deerfield Beach, FL: Health Communications, Inc., 1997.

Carnes, P. *Out of the Shadows: Understanding Sexual Addiction.* Center City, MN: Hazelden Publishing, 2001.

Carnes, S., Lee, M., & Rodriguez, A. *Facing Heartbreak: Steps to Recovery for Partners of Sex Addicts.* Carefree, AZ: Gentle Path Press, 2012.

Crane, J. *The Trauma Heart*. Deerfield Beach, FL: Health Communications, Inc., 2017.

Ferree, M. *No Stones: Women Redeemed From Sexual Addiction*. Downers Grove, IL: InterVarsity Press, 2010.

Johnson, S. *Love Sense: The Revolutionary New Science of Romantic Relationships*. New York, NY: Little, Brown and Company, 2013.

Katehakis, A. *Mirror of Intimacy: Daily Reflections on Emotional and Erotic Intelligence*. Los Angeles, CA: Center for Healthy Sex, 2014

Katehakis, A. *Erotic Intelligence: Igniting Hot, Healthy Sex While in Recovery from Sex Addiction*. Deerfield Beach, FL: Health Communications, Inc., 2010.

Katehakis, A. *Sex Addiction as Affect Dysregulation: A Neurobiologically Informed Holistic Treatment*. New York, NY: W.W. Norton & Co., Inc., 2016.

Levine, P. *In an Unspoken Voice: How the Body Releases Trauma and Restores Goodness*. Berkeley, CA: North Atlantic Books, 2010.

Levine, P. & Kline, M. *Trauma Through a Child's Eyes: Awakening the Ordinary Miracle of Healing: Infancy through Adolescence*. Berkeley, CA: North Atlantic Books, 2006.

Levine, P. *Waking the Tiger: Healing Trauma*. Berkeley, CA: North Atlantic Books, 1997.

Lipton, B. *The Biology of Belief: Unleashing the Power of Consciousness, Matter & Miracles*. Carlsbad, CA: Hay House, Inc., 2015.

Matè, G. *In the Realm of Hungry Ghosts: Close Encounters with Addiction.* Berkeley, CA: North Atlantic Books, 2010.

Matè, G. *When the Body Says No: Understanding the Stress-Disease Connection.* Hoboken, NJ: John Wiley & Sons, 2003.

Mellody, P., Miller, A., & Miller, K. *Facing Love Addiction: Giving Yourself the Power to Change the Way You Love.* San Francisco, CA: Harper, 2003.

Mellody, P., Freundlich, L. *The Intimacy Factor: The Ground Rules for Overcoming the Obstacles to Truth, Respect, and Lasting Love.* San Francisco: Harper, 2004.

Miller, A. *The Drama of the Gifted Child: The Search for the True Self.* New York, NY: Basic Books, 2007.

Miller, A. & Jenkins, A. *For Your Own Good: Hidden Cruelty in Child Rearing and the Roots of Violence.* New York: The Noonday Press, 1990.

Miller, A. *The Truth Will Set You Free: Overcoming Emotional Blindness and Finding Your True Adult Self.* New York: Basic Books, 2002.

Real, T. *I Don't Want to Talk About It.* New York: Simon & Schuster, Inc., 1998.

Real, T. *The New Rules of Marriage: What You Need to Know to Make Love Work.* New York: Ballantine Books, 2008.

Siegel, D. *Mind: A Journey to the Heart of Being Human.* New York, NY: Norton, 2017.

Siegel, D. *Mindsight: The New Science of Personal Transformation.* New York, NY: Bantam Trade Paperbacks, 2011.

Siegel, D. *The Mindful Brain: Reflection and Attunement in the Cultivation of Wellbeing.* New York, NY: W.W. Norton, 2007.

Siegel, D. & Solomon, M. *Healing Trauma: Attachment, Mind, Body and Brain.* New York, NY: Norton, 2003.

Sprout, S. *Naked in Public: A Memoir of Recovery from Sex Addiction and Other Temporary Insanities.* Seattle, WA: Recontext Media, LLC, 2015.

Tatkin, S. *Wired for Love.* Oakland, CA: New Harbinger Publications, Inc., 2011.

Tidwell Palmer, V. *Moving Beyond Betrayal: The 5-Step Boundary Solution for Partners of Sex Addicts.* Las Vegas, NV: Central Recovery Press, 2016.

Van der Kolk, B. *The Body Keeps the Score.* New York: Penguin Books, 2014.

Weiss, R. *Prodependence: Moving Beyond Codependency.* Deerfield Beach, FL: Health Communications, Inc., 2018.

Weiss, R. *Cruise Control: Understanding Sex Addiction in Gay Men.* Carefree, AZ: Gentle Path Press, 2013.

Weiss, R. *Out of the Doghouse: A Step by Step Relationship-Saving Guide for Men Caught Cheating.* Deerfield Park, FL: Health Communications, Inc., 2017.

Van der Kolk, B. *The Body Keeps the Score.* New York: Penguin Books, 2014.

Zukav, G. *Spiritual Partnership: The Journey to Authentic Power.* New York: HarperCollins, 2010.

Index

bodywork, 124–125
couples' work, 144–147
Dialectical Behavior Therapy (DBT),
   122–123
Eye Movement Desensitization and
   Reprocessing (EMDR), 125–126
medication and, 121–122
Mindfulness-Based Stress Reduction
   (MBSR), 127–128
Radically Open Dialectical Behavior
   Therapy (RO-DBT), 123
resources for, 129
Somatic Experiencing (SE), 127
talk therapy, 122
yoga, 128

Q
quality time, need for, 133–138

R
Radically Open Dialectical Behavior
   Therapy (RO-DBT), 123
resources, 177–183
   body awareness techniques, 177–179
   12-step programs, 181–182
respect
   of boundaries, 152–153
   understanding, 155–157
right brain, 41–45
Rohr, Richard, 59

S
safety in relationships, 137–140
scapegoating behavior, 6, 80, 95, 151
Self. *See also* consciousness; mindfulness meditation; spiritual abuse
   conscious mind and, 61–63
   defined, xv, 11
   knowing true Self for healing, 65–69
   Self-realization, 59
   stories and effect on, xvii

"Separation Anxiety" (Bowlby), 36
sexual abuse
   defined, 10
   physical and sexual boundaries,
      148–149
   by religious representatives, 16
sexual activity
   in healthy relationships, 140–144
   infidelity and, 24
   living in balance and, 118
   physical and sexual boundaries for,
      148–149
sexual orientation, 55–59
shame, sex and, 142–144
Shapiro, Francine, 125–126
siblings
   with high needs, 4–6, 23
   parents' focus on one sibling's
      achievements, 24
simplifying your life, 101–105
   listing activities for, 103–104
   need for, 101–103
   simplifying your space for, 104–105
single parents, 24
social media, 108–109
spiritual abuse
   defined, 11
   false empowerment as, 12–13
   harmful religious behavior as, 15–19
   parent as Higher Power to child,
      11–12
   physical/emotional/sexual abuse by
      religious representatives, 16
*Spiritual Dimension of the Enneagram,
   The* (Maitri), 61–62
spirituality
   connecting with people at spiritual
      venues, 110
   staying in the now and teachings
      of, 99
   symbols for, *169*, 169–172, *171*

Made in the USA
Monee, IL
05 January 2022

88028115R00122